THE GIFT OF
KEVIN

AS WRITTEN BY
MELODI SHIPLEY

Melod Shipley

Michelle Andrews

Senior editor/It consultant

Connor Shipley

editor

Print ISBN: 978-1-66786-513-3

eBook ISBN: 978-1-66786-514-0

IN LOVING MEMORY

I dedicate this book to my beloved son
Kevin Tyler Shipley
I am honored to be your mom
I am so blessed to have you as my son
You will be forever in our hearts.

To my loving husband David,
Thank you for all your support and
Always being there for us. We love you.

To our other amazing son,
Connor for being the best son
a mother could ever dream of.

We are so proud of our sons,
and the eternal unbreakable bond we share.
Everything we've endured so far has led me
to believe that our love will never die.

The four of us are forever, just like the innocent
Love a red rose symbolizes. I love my family and
I cannot thank God enough for their presence in
my life.

ACKNOWLEDGMENTS

Writing a book is harder than I thought and more rewarding than I could have ever possibly imagined.None of this would have been possible without my beautiful niece Michelle Andrews.

When she heard the tragic news, she stopped everything in her life to be by my side. She stayed with me the whole time.

I couldn't function, she assisted me, she protected me, and she stood by me during the struggle I had losing my oldest son. I am internally grateful for her she not only is my niece she is my editor and IT specialist for this book.

She is incredible, her experience in the computer world fit right in. I needed to get this message out-and she organized my computer and stepped up to the plate on knowing everything on how to formulate my experiences into a book.

I wrote the journal, and we worked together on making this book come true.

When I first asked her for help, I knew she'd be the perfect person…. because when she was a young girl, she used to write poems to me, her Aunt Melodi. I loved every single one of them.

God bless you I love you with all my heart.

The way I believe is that most of our life is pre-planned out the way we choose it to be. God knew that I would need some angels down here on earth when it came time for my son to go back home.

God created and blessed me with six beautiful, caring, and loving Angels.

He knew they would take care of me and give me
strength and comfort when I needed it the most.
These angels carried me when I couldn't walk.
They held me in their arms to let me
know they were never going to leave my side.
They stepped into my darkest hour and shined their lights to help me make it through,

Thank you, dear God, for sending me these heavenly angels

Charlie & Connie Karadimos "Kevin's God Parents"

Michelle Andrews

Margret Kernan

Cara May

Kim Cicchino

I BELIEVE IN ANGELS

The world is a better place with family and friends especially the ones I have.

My heart was overwhelmed with all the thoughtful gifts, beautiful flowers, plants, sympathy cards, visits to my home, phone calls, delicious food and even the special thinking of you text messages.

I'm so deeply blessed with compassionate and thoughtful people that surround us all the time.

I love each and every one of you.
Thank you all.
God bless you.

Honoring in memory of
Kevin Tyler Shipley

A good friend of Kevin's named his son's middle name after Kevin's middle name
Cameron Tyler Francella.

My great niece named her son
Kaleb Harris
A Jewish tradition.
They take the first letter of someone they love who has passed away (Kevin) and name a new baby beginning with that letter.

CONTENTS

INTRODUCTION

There are many unfortunate instances that one must go through in life, many that are insignificant enough that you don't even remember a few hours later, and many that can be easily dealt with to remove all the consequences of it.

However, some such incidents are so impactful and troubling that even after you've done your best to deal with the damage, even after you've spent years in pain, from its affect, you still wouldn't be able to move past it and run the course of your life like you previously did.

One of such incidences is the passing of a loved one.

From what I believe and have experienced in my life it is the most challenging thing that one must deal with. It is a pain that I wish no one must go through ever. If only, wishes could reverse it.

My son, Kevin was the most blessed thing to ever walk in my life. 10 years after my marriage, after I struggled so long to conceive, I was rewarded with Kevin as a result of in-vitro fertilization. After praying for a child for so long, you best believe I did all I could in my ability to give him the best life I was able to and to make him happy and look after him as a mother should

But as love would have it, he was taken away from me too soon and my bright and happy life was turned into one continuous never-ending heartbroken day.

It was then when I felt the real, terrifying, and agonizing pain of losing my loving son Kevin. It was a pain I've never experienced before.

My life turned upside down. Even though Kevin was the one that left the world. I was the one that stopped living.

I was angry at the world. I was angry at God. The same God that had blessed me with the gift of a child and had taken away that gift from me way too soon. Then something changed.

A month after his passing I started to re-open my soul and my mind up to all the possibilities. I became more in tune with the spirit world around me.

First it started with signs from the other side that only Kevin's brother, father and I would ever know.

This brought not only comfort but a deeper understanding of life after death. Little did I know this would open me up to a beautiful and mysterious new world.

It was the most healing experience.

Kevin's life had been a gift to me while he was alive and now, he is giving me gifts from the other side too.

It was then when I realized that what I had brought into this world as my son Kevin was way closer to the perfect love that every soul wants and is trying to get to.

Kevin had been a blessing in our lives. You can never see it coming. None of us can. When life takes away what you love most, you feel like your whole world is ripped apart.

I had always believed that raising my sons to the best they can be was my purpose in life but now I realized it has changed and now it is to share with you a personal experience connected with life here on earth and life beyond physical death.

I want to tell you that there is a better way to deal with life's hardest obstacles. There is a way you can still be connected to your loved ones even in the afterlife. It would help if you kept your mind and soul open to the possibilities because they are endless. Being hopeless is not the way to be. This is not the way your loved ones would have wanted you to live. You do not have to waste away the rest of your life here on earth or live the rest of your life without purpose.

Whoever is out there reading this, I hope this book helps you deal with loss of life and opens your mind up to fully recognize the beautiful signs you'll experience from loved ones on the other side. I want to tell you about my journey and the wonders of the place, I call heaven.

All of it is very real. You just have to believe

PREFACE

Michelle and I are finally here in my home office getting ready to work on the "The gift of Kevin". This has been planned for a couple of weeks now. We are finally here; healing music is playing in the background. We have incense burning; it's a calm and quiet atmosphere in my office – very peaceful. I am telling my niece Michelle how deeply sad and devastated I am on losing personal text messages between my son Kevin and me.

After Kevin 's passing, Connor had taken Kevin's cell phone. Every time I would visit Connor, I would look through Kevin's messages to feel closer to him. There were years' worth of Personal conversations that he had saved between him and me. It made me feel, he was still alive and closer to him when I would read those conversations. I would cry and cry and cry, every time I would read them.

Recently, it came to be that my husband needed a new phone, so we thought we would get the phone from Connor, and he can use Kevin 's phone.

Now, with Kevin's phone back in my possession, I was looking forward to reading even more of those messages again.

A few days ago, I went into my office to read our messages and that is when I saw the messages were gone. I was devastated; I couldn't believe that they got deleted. These text messages were very important to me as you can imagine.

As we are talking about this, and slowly concluding that it was maybe a blessing in disguise; Kevin's way of saying 'let go mom and move on'. In the quiet out of nowhere we hear a loud thump. At that moment my niece and I looked at each other and she said a black bird just hit the window. I ran outside to see if the bird had died or flew away. When I checked, there was no bird, it had flown away.

In those moments, we knew it was a sign. There was no question. My niece looked up the meaning of a black bird hitting the window and flying off and this is what it said.

> *"At times, birds hit the window carrying a message that we need to overcome obstacles*
>
> *I will say that you should not mistake this as physical death. Some books do say that it represents transition.*
>
> *Remember, when one door closes, another one opens for you.*
>
> *So, the bird could be closing one door in your life and opening another one. It could be that there is going to be an end to the suffering* **now time to heal yourself."**

MOTHER

I Am a Mother of Life

I Am a Mother of Loss

I Am Grief

I Have Grief

Therefore, I Am Alive

I Feel

I Am Matter

I Matter

We Are All Made Up of Matter

We All Are in The Same Reality

With Different Paths

I Will Share Mine…

CHAPTER 1

THE RED ROSE

As you read this chapter you will come to find out what the Red Rose symbolizes to me.

It's February 14, 1975, Valentine's Day I'll be 16 soon and David, my boyfriend, is on his way over. He's taking me out to dinner. I was beyond excited. He made me feel something I've never felt before. Even on Valentine's Day he managed to sweep me right off my feet with a dozen of long-stemmed red roses, a sentimental Valentine card, and a box of chocolates. It was all so dreamy and beautiful.

We ended up becoming High school sweethearts.

Little did I know at the time the Rose was a symbol. A symbol that love, lasts forever, and can never die; instead, it gives birth to an eternal unbreakable bond. To me they were just beautiful red roses. What they would come to mean in my life later on was something I could not comprehend then.

I was brought up in the Catholic faith.

I sang in the choir when I was a young girl every Sunday at church.

I did holy communion, CCD classes and confirmation.

I was raised in a time where you graduated from high school, you got married, had babies, and that was living the dream. Everything else was a bonus.

On May 9, 1981, David and I got married. We had a beautiful Catholic wedding. A few years went by, and we decided it was time to start our family.

We tried all throughout 1985 to 1986, with no pregnancy. Despite the repeated fails, we didn't lose hope. In 1987, I finally got pregnant, but unfortunately it was an ectopic pregnancy. Then another ectopic in 1990. More disappointment came through, as a result, I suffered a loss of my fallopian tubes. Now, the only way I could get pregnant was through a new technology called in-vitro fertilization. It was very expensive, and most insurance companies did not cover any of it.

We went to the in-vitro consultation and put $10,000 down for only one try.

To my surprise, the very next day, at work, HR sent a letter out to everyone, it was on my desk as well. It was an amendment from our health insurance company.

A miracle had struck.

My health insurance is now paying for in-vitro procedures for 3 tries! Also, if I gave birth out of one of those 3 tries, I earn 3 more. I ran down to the HR office to see if this was really true. I was in such shock/ disbelief; I needed to see if I was reading this correctly.

The probability of something like this happening around the same time we needed this the most was next to zero, yet the universe was siding with us.

It is with this miracle, that began The Gift of Kevin.

We got our 10 grand back from the consultation and the journey of conception finally began.

But still my beliefs held strong as after every hurdle, God opened a new path for us, and blessed us in the most surprising and beautiful ways possible. Despite having 2 ectopic pregnancies and 2 unsuccessful in-vitro procedures, David and I kept trying. I wasn't going to give up. I was determined that having a baby was my purpose, and all I ever wanted in life was a family of my own.

I used to cry at every baby shower I went to, and I used to wonder why conceiving wasn't as easy for us as it was for other people. Later, I realized it was because God wanted to bless us with Kevin.

My miracle happened. Kevin was conceived on the third try and born at 3:52 AM, on October 16, 1991.

Though he came into this world a little earlier than his due date, Kevin was a healthy baby, he weighed 5 lbs. 13 oz. was 19 1/2 inches long.

When I first held my baby in my arms, I couldn't believe he was real. That sweet and innocent face was all that I had ever wanted to hold in my arms. It seemed too good to be true. I had waited so long for it and there were so many sad tears along the way, but I finally got blessed with the most beautiful baby in my eyes.

I was complete, he was mine.

I loved Kevin when he was a dream, a wish, and a hope. I loved Kevin from the moment he was inside my belly, and I will keep loving him until my last breath. From all the time that we had spent together, I felt a special bond between Kevin and me. A special love that I had never felt for anyone. I finally had my purpose in life. It took a little time, but he was finally here, and I was not going to let go.

He was such a beautiful baby. Even my neighbor thought so much so that he used Kevin as his model in an ad for a pediatrics magazine; Kevin laying on a baby scale. He sold baby scales to doctors' offices and hospitals. Kevin was a family celebrity!

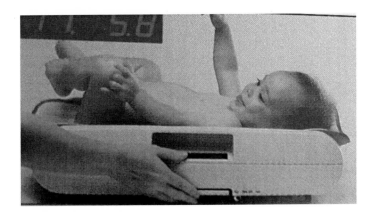

As a toddler, he chose his love for wrestling. David and I were channel-surfing one evening and WWF came up on one of the stations while we were switching channels. He yelled," Mommy stop, go back! go back!"

We said," What? Back to this?"

Kevin gave a small nod, and with an adorable smile, said, "*Me like that*".

That's when he became a WWF fan forever. He had all the wrestling men figures, the ring, the belt. You name it, he had it. Every day with him was like an exciting new adventure.

He would play with his toys, and he would follow me from room to room as I did my daily household chores. He always wanted to be aware of where I was, so he could always stay close to me. Every night I would read him his beloved bedtime stories. He wouldn't go to sleep without them. I loved being around him. I would also sing to him because he liked it whenever I sang, unlike other people who hear my voice. He also sang with me during our car rides. He came to love singing so much that he would even sing himself to sleep

Music was Kevin 's passion. He had an unbelievable amount of knowledge about all the different genres of music. When Kevin was 2 years old, we were expecting another baby from in-vitro. We asked him if he wanted a baby brother or baby sister and he always said he wanted baby *"butter"*. No matter how many times we asked him.

Then the time came when we welcomed a new baby boy named Connor. Kevin got what he wanted a Baby "butter". The two boys were inseparable and had this eternal unbreakable bond with each other. They were built in playmates; they played all the time. The love that they have between each other was unbelievable and a thing to envy for many. I guess you can call them twins, as they both were conceived at the same time with Connor being one of the frozen embryos.

They always seemed to know what the other one was thinking without saying anything.

I shared with you, some of my precious memories of Kevin. Now he will share with you, in his own words his Autobiography.

KEVIN'S SENIOR AUTOBIOGRAPHY

My name is Kevin Tyler Shipley, and I was born into this world on October 16, 1991 in Columbia Maryland. I have a family of four, which consists of my mother (Melodi), father (David), and brother (Connor). Life in Maryland was great, we had a huge backyard which was a playground and every day we had friends and neighbors over playing and running around. WWF was big back then and my family would all order PP V's and enjoy us some Stone Cold(wrestler). It wasn't until 2004, when we moved to West Virginia and started another chapter in my life. Life changed, and I started over from scratch making new friends and adapting to a new school system. When starting my new journey in West Virginia, I made new friends and continued onward. I attended Hedgesville Middle School, where I made the honor roll on each and every report card and even got a Citizenship Award for academic achievement. From there I began High school at Hedgesville High School, and I participated in Football my Freshman and Sophomore years and Track, respectively. I currently am swimming for the high school and am going to States. Let me tell you something, I'm a first-year swimmer and I'm already beating people who've been a part of swimming their whole life. Sometimes I wonder how I am so fast. It must be my muscles since I am built like a Herculean gladiator. But aside from sports being my success, my academic excellence also excelled to greater heights in high school. I became an Eagle S.O.A.R (Student Outstanding Academic Recognition) Award winner not once, but three times, plus I have achieved the ultimate goal of Faithful Attendance, which is not missing too many days of school. By doing so you get a free Domino's Pizza at the end of the year, and last time I checked Dominos is good, so I think I'll take this deal. I am also a champion when it comes to making Honor Roll. My 4.0 GPA doesn't speak for itself, through hard work and dedication I have showed my knack for comprehending topics. Throughout school I have been privileged to have been a part of many classes that have motivated me and one that comes to mind is Mr. DiNicola's Marketing class. This wasn't your average class, the activities taught and learned did not only impact me, it also impacted the community. Upon joining this class, you automatically are in the club DECA. This club helps in community projects. WE have impacted the community in several ways by either doing trash pickup or fundraising money for the March of Dimes, which, to go on record, I participated in and not only enjoyed it but proceeded to kick my teachers rear in the actual race. Five miles to be exact, so thank you track. However, none can compare to the annual DECA Christmas Party for underprivileged kids. The DECA group and I get a select few of children and go shop for them. Then we follow it up with a Christmas party in their honor. This is one of the greatest moments I have done, it really gives you the concept of its better to give than receive, and I loved every minute of it. DECA is a life-changing club and I have become an advocate for other high school kids to join. I have also been proactive in helping my school and the community in sporting events. I have helped line football fields, record stats for teams, mop and clean wrestling mats and equipment. I also work in the school store, where I proudly serve the students. I have gained a lot of life lessons from Hedgesville and will be a proud Alumni.

Education is important to me and through all my accomplishments, I have shown all the hard work and dedication I put forth, to pursue the most of each experience. It paid off when Shepherd University accepted me into their college. While attending Shepherd University, I plan to obtain a degree in Marketing with a minor in Education. I do have many goals for myself, like educating myself in efforts to pursue my true calling in life. I also want to get my bachelor's degree, and continuing all my high school goals, like continuing my community service work and keep my 4.0 going strong. As for long term goals, I would hope to pursue a career in which helps me grow as a person each day just like my high school and soon college experiences have done. While my future holds bright, in the present I'm still enjoying life day in and day out, whether it be singing songs in the shower, going to grab wings with my friends at Buffalo Wild Wings; I'm just keeping the memories so I can reflect back on them later in life, and to tell my children someday. Though I don't recommend them to jump off cliffs higher than sixty-plus feet. This just reflects on my daredevil like personality. Maybe after all those darn days spent inside Gold's Gym; I lost my conscious. Yet only time will tell, what Kevin's life will turn out. Hopefully my leadership and speaking skills will land me a job as a teacher or a Marketing specialist. Either way you have it, my life will be a happy one, and I will seize the day.

Like Robin Williams said in The Dead Poets Society, Carpe Diem!

CHAPTER 2

DOWN MEMORY LANE

KEVIN'S EULOGY —
WRITTEN AND SPOKEN AT HIS MEMORIAL
BY HIS BROTHER, CONNOR SHIPLEY

Let's look around the room. I want you to see how strong and how deep the love for Kevin Tyler Shipley is. I want you to see how a loving, funny, charismatic, and generous individual can shine light on so many lives. You can feel it all around you. Kevin loves every single one of you, and I love everyone too.

Let's take a trip down memory lane.

Kevin was 160 pounds of twisted steel and sex appeal when he ran a 4.4 forty-yard dash on the concrete. He was a natural athlete. The first time he ever touched a football, in the first game of his career, in the very first play of the season, he went 75 yards for a touchdown. My dad also went 75 yards for a touchdown on the sidelines.

Kevin played adult hockey league. He bought his equipment, laced up his skates, and tried something new. Despite no prior skating experience, Kevin still managed to get a hat trick. He would score in the sloppiest of ways, like literally falling sometimes. Kevin also celebrated each goal. Some of the celebrations were so over the top, from riding the stick like a horse to something completely ignorant, Kevin was a show in himself. Kevin loved playing hockey. I felt honored to be his teammate.

In school, Kevin was loved by his teachers, classmates, and coaches. He was a two-sport state qualifier, and state finalist. Kevin could achieve any goal he set out to accomplish, and in doing so, he made sure he had to put in minimal effort or like faking a hamstring injury for a few weeks to get out of track practice.

The funny thing about Kevin was that when he came home after qualifying for a state track meet unlike most kids the only thing Kevin could think about was two more weeks of practice.

Well, practice paid off, and Kevin became a state runner-up, and his relay team meddled.

One of my fondest sports memories with Kevin is the swim team, the trips, the funny moments, and the friends we made.

In the time trials of the first meet after not swimming in years, he stood up in the pool to catch his breath while swimming the IM.

Literally stood up middle of the pool to catch his breath. Of course, Kevin made it to the states. Kevin and I got to swim together, and with all the pressure surrounding us, Kevin got his best time he's ever had and set the leg off strong for our relay.

The only other faster time on our relay was me.

If we're talking about sports, I need to mention how big a Titans fan my brother is. I'm talking walking around the house with the Titans blanket on—what a funny team.

The heartbreak, along with the games they managed to win including the funny drama surrounding them, got us to witness Kevin during football season, which was a ton of laughter. I mean, literally, the Titans would dictate his mood sometimes. If they lost, he would say, "I am done with football for the day," and not watch any of the other games. Didn't matter if it was a 1 pm game.

Kevin, you are literally such a character. I know you're here right now brother, with God and with us. So, for those two as my witness, I declare myself a Titans' Fan.

Growing up with Kevin, we loved our wrestling. I'm talking about Vince McMahon, WWF, WWE, more specifically, the attitude era. From trying moves on one another in our homemade ring in the basement in Columbia, Maryland, to watching Pay Per Views with the lifeguards at the pool, who were in high school while Kevin and I were just seven and five. Kevin and I were the coolest little kids, giving each other Stone Cold stunners, suplexes, powerbombs, and the occasional frog splash, all while telling one another that I got two words for you. "Suck it!!"

Though to all of us right now, this feels like rock bottom. We will only go up from here. Kevin, you are the perfect example of what being yourself looks like. You were so genuine to all.

Kevin didn't see age. He treated everyone with respect and was never "too cool" to hang out with my mom and dad's friends. You all are Kevin's friends. Kevin looked you in the eyes when he would speak to you. His words had meaning, and when he spoke, one would best listen to him. It has been very remarkable and touching over the past couple of days, hearing how you have impacted the lives of so many individuals, Kevin. I have heard so many stories this past week from people. Stories ranging from you helping a friend grieve the loss of his father, to the joy you were to work with at all your jobs, to lending a helping hand to any friend when they needed one, As well as the typical hilarious Kevin story that embodies your character.

I am going to say five names, and I want you to rank them from immature to most immature". All these stories have one thing in common: you are, and were so loved, and more importantly, had so much love to give. These memories illustrate the pure soul our Kevin has. These stories will carry us through a hard time.

I HAVE TO PRAISE YOU
LIKE I SHOULD

Kevin is so funny without trying. I mean, Kevin is so, so, so funny. He will forever make me laugh. I could name a trillion things he's done. From the improv comedy sketches, to your witty comebacks, to your wild imagination. Your impersonations are unreal. I like to recognize a time when, as a family, we sat down for our game night to play apples for apples.

The hilarious cards you would put and the synergy we had to know whose card is whose.

Kevin, the long personalized messages that you sent me all the time would brighten my day and give me the strength to conquer the unknown. Nobody can make me feel the way you do.

He sent me songs that captured the perfect emotion to reflect on life, be inspired, laugh, or go. Kevin, what the heck was that? These songs ranged from every genre always good. Kevin had such a love and passion for music. He went through every type of headphone; his collection of music was so insanely vast. Kevin and I loved going to see live music together. We would pack up the car and hit the road. All these road trips and adventures we took have filled my heart. On one trip, we drove all the way down to Alabama for New Year's Eve. Let's just say Kevin did most of the driving. I did get you back on Ohio one though! One moment I'd Love to share was at a place called Camp Bisco. The freedom of being on the mountain and camping with one another was surreal! Brian gets lost, Kev goes, "I'll get lost now".

Mom and Dad let me tell you this right now, you raised a wonderful man. We have the strongest tight-knit group of four, and our bond cannot and will not be broken. Kevin had all the wonderful features, that some families pray their kids would just have one of those qualities.

Kevin was never afraid to express his love to family, friends, or even complete strangers. Kevin always made sure he told his family he loved them. Whether it be a big hug and kiss for his mom in public, at school, or in front of all his friends. He made sure he expressed his true feelings. Dad, the way Kevin would describe your bond and how you guys hung out, I have to say you guys are best friends. And Dad, if you look around you, you got a bunch of young men who think the world of you. And for anybody out there, if you were coming to visit, best believe Kevin would hug you and welcome you with open arms to the Shipley household.

I am Kevin, (Kev is my twin as we were conceived through in-vitro and I was the frozen one., so we come from the same batch for lack of better terms). Kevin and I shared everything together. We influenced one another.

Explained our third eye, intuition, similar Love for everything.

But the way I see it, Kevin, you shaped my entire life. Everything I am because of you. I got to look up to you, I got to watch you grow, and most importantly, I got the chance to have a Big Brother who loved me.

I wish I could tell the world how much you have impacted my life, but a room full of family, friends, and loved ones works just as well. Instead, what I'm going to do is show the world my character, attitude, and outlook on life. I will show how strong our love is and how inseparable we are.

Kevin aspired to explore the outdoors, participate in variety of new and exciting sports. He wanted to open water swim in the freshwater. He wanted to hike mountains and explore the outdoors. Kevin loved being in nature. I remember, when we all went cliff-jumping in the Riverbend, Kevin jumped off a 75-foot cliff in the river. Not just once either. We loved going there with our friends and playing in the Potomac. Or the trips to Ocean City, in which we would pray for a storm so the waves would get heavy and rough. Those were always the most fun to swim in. Kevin also really wanted to participate in a triathlon. It consisted of swimming, biking, and running. He has been working out multiple days a week. He bought a bike suit, when he was buying a bike and had just recently purchased a full body wetsuit. Kevin had told me he wanted to move out to Colorado in May. He had so many dreams in life.

Kevin passed away last Thursday.

You have given me such an abundance of LOVE, HAPPINESS, LAUGHTER, KNOWLEDGE, CONFIDENCE, and BROTHERHOOD.

I will live every day on God's green earth to the fullest. Kevin, you came to me last Friday at 6:00 am. When my father delivered the news, I fell to the kitchen floor. My heart exploded, poured out of my chest. You didn't want to see your little brother so hurt, you comforted me.

I will forget the feeling of my heart pouring out of my chest. But I will never forget the feeling of you soothing me when I stood up and walked towards the window. From there I looked out into the city skies. I felt it all. I saw a glimpse of our future. Kevin you were there with me. You showed me our vision.

I felt your strength. I felt your love. I felt *you.*

From that day on, I knew we were one. We will conquer our dreams down here on this playground. All the while smelling the roses because life on earth as we know is temporary. But eternal life and eternal love are forever and ever. I feel you.

Energy cannot be created nor destroyed. Kevin together, we are going to see the world together, we are going to keep trucking. We have dreams to chase. Your love is forever with me. Your strength is forever with me. Your light shines forever through me. I will share this glory with all I see…

I LOVE YOU FOREVER AND ALWAYS, MY BIG BROTHER,
MY BEST FRIEND, MY ANGEL

Those were my words when I couldn't speak. Those were my words when I couldn't eat. Those were my words when an hour felt like an eternity. I lost my big brother and my best friend on March 7th 2019.I received a call from my father at 6am March 8th 2019. That same day I had to fly home 4 ½ hours-sit there in my own head knowing when I land, I won't see him. Instead, I'm going to see my mom and my dad and Kevin's dog Stella. How do you stay strong when the ones who are supposed to stay strong are broken? How does one comfort another when they too are broken? I don't know…but you must.

CHAPTER 3

GRIEVING

KEVIN TYLER SHIPLEY
10/16/1991 − 03/07/2019

The cause of death was asphyxiation. Due to practicing neck compressions that turn into a fatal accident.

I started writing a personal journal documenting every supernatural and extraordinary experience of the beyond, and even my grieving.

Everything I have experienced I have kept record of in my journal raw format. My journal now has become my book, I will share these stories with you.

Grieving comes in all different forms.

Every day I grieve, in some way. You never really know how you're going to feel when you wake up. You just get through it day by day.

I wake up crying and grieving for my son. I was trying to meditate and pray because I needed God's help to calm myself down.

The holidays are here, and each day is such a struggle.

My son Kevin loved the holidays. We always went out and did things together during the season.

He appreciated everything I did to make the Christmas season a merry and bright one. We loved seeing the decorations, baking cookies, shopping, and watching Christmas movies and shows.

I was having a moment and could not stop crying. I needed help.

Then suddenly I heard Stella,

Kevin's dog, yelp from downstairs.

She does that when she's upset or scared.

I went running downstairs to see what was wrong. I realized at that moment that God had sent me the help that I needed. There was my sign.

Holding Stella brought me comfort. She took my mind from my grief and turned it to loving her.

Sometimes when you are grieving, signs come around, we will talk more about signs in chapter 4.

Life is different for me now.

Still, despite these differences, I need to find my path.

The path that I have been on for a long time has ended.

A New Year will be here soon. It will now be two years since Kevin has passed away.

It's time for me to make changes. Help me, dear God, my angels, and my guardian angel,

Kevin, I love you.

My new purpose is what lies ahead of me. The person I was and the person I am are now crossing paths.

Things have changed.

I have changed.

I am broken inside.

You just don't get glued back together again just like that.

You struggle every day, wishing for a better ending.

But somehow it doesn't seem to get any better. You know you have to get up and get moving because you have to complete your purpose.

You have a husband and son here that need you.

And you need them.

Your family and friends love you.

Still, despite all that, there are days when I don't want to get up.

Who wants to clean?

Not me.

You lay in bed and think and no matter what your mind and heart process, the outcome is still the same.

You're not a person anymore, you're an abstraction, a wave of grief that overpowers everything. Above everything else, you miss your son.

No one can help you with that

I was very close to my son Kevin. He was not only my son; we were also terrific friends.

He loved hanging out with his dad and me. We would go shopping and dine out.

When we would have gatherings with our friends, he would invite all of his friends over and we'd all hang out together.

He would hang out with his dad every Friday by the pool. It was their thing, they "chilled" every weekend. It was Happy Hour Time together to talk and listen to good music.

They would get out the speakers and crank them up. They would light the tiki lights, citronella candle and crack open a ice cold beer.

It was their special thing. My husband looked forward to Fridays with his son.

Now it's all gone.

Fridays are not special anymore. Just another day missing your son.

My family is remarkably close and filled with love for one another. He was the type of son who would hug and kiss me every time he saw me, no matter where I was. Even in front of his friends. He didn't care. He loved his mother so much and he wasn't afraid to show it.

Every day he would say, "I love you mom."

Every now and then, he would say, "Mom, I didn't get my hug and kiss today". He was my everything, and then he died just like that no warnings, no nothing.

After Kevin passed, we had to tell our son Connor. He lives in Colorado, so we had to make the phone call, instead of telling him face to face.

The worst thing we had to do was tell him that Kevin had died over the phone. There was no other way. We had to get Connor home.

I prayed all day for God to get him home safely.

I wake up every day and I am in a nightmare. My life is a nightmare.

I'm in jail; I'm not free; I'm a prisoner of my pain. I have no energy to push myself. Every day is a struggle to get up knowing I will never see my son again on this earth.

I just couldn't let my mind think of the future. I felt like I was being punished. I didn't feel like being around people. I had stopped socializing on the internet. I didn't want to speak or text anybody. I felt uncomfortable inside. I'm broken. I feel numb. I know there is nothing else that could hurt me so deeply in my lifetime. I'm living the worst nightmare and can't wake up from it. There will never be any waking up from it. It is my reality now.

The only thing that makes me survive is that I have to be here for Connor and David.

I go to bed crying. I wake up with tears streaming down my face.

There is no relief. Every cell in my body and mind, and heart is in mourning and in pain.

Why did this have to happen? Why did this have to happen to me? To us? There is nothing that makes sense about losing a child. I am so unhappy I can't even fake that I'm not. I don't want to be around anyone. It's not fair. Why? Why?

When I am around people, I hold everything in until I'm alone and then I can release all my emotions.

Emotions I had never felt before. Emotions I didn't know existed until I lost my son. There is no waking up from this bad dream that I'm living.

I prayed all the time to God to watch over my boys. I was not afraid of death. I knew God was taking care of us. But what happened, this was not supposed to happen.

Dear God, where are you?

Were my prayers not answered?

My boys were my purpose here on earth. I went through pain and heartaches to have my two beautiful boys, and now, one of them dies, in a split second, my life is over. Where was God? Where were the angels? Who was supposed to be watching over my son!?

Everything I believed in didn't exist anymore. I am left with a broken heart and no purpose anymore. Life is not fun. I am lost in this world. The world as I know it is gone.

03/07/2020

I got up to go get dressed, then the phone rang. It was one of Kevin's friends. He said some of the guys want to come over if that's alright. We said absolutely come on over. They all came over to be with us on the 1 year of Kevin's passing.

We went up to Kevin's room. I lit some candles in his room by his picture. I also had a candle lit on the dining room table downstairs for Kevin. It was a good atmosphere.

We took some pictures together. The boys stayed up there for a little bit to reminisce. Then we all drank some beer and talked about Kevin. Everyone had a story to tell.

Everybody so loved my son.

We miss you so much, Kevin.

I hope you don't mind, but we will grieve you for the rest of our lives.

You are very important to us. We will never stop loving you. You are our family you completed us

"The Shipley's."

Life is hard without you.

We cry every day, but they are tears of love.

You have shown us how to love and what love is all about.

We will learn to cope, and we know, that we have to complete our journey here, and we will. It's not going to be easy, but for you, we will survive.

I will keep searching and learning about the other side where you are at because I want to still be a part of your life.

I will never let you go.

I will be with you on both sides. God has given me a gift. Thank you, dear God, I love you.

As grief took over everything in my
life, I realized that I needed my
Mommy.

She is the greatest Mother that I could ever ask for, she was always there for me no matter what. She would comfort me with her positive beliefs. She would make me feel like everything will be alright and I always believe her, because she was always right.

She is 88 years old and has dementia.

I thought I would try to talk to her, because I really needed my Mom, I asked her,

"Mom, what do we believe in?"

She said, "Well we are born, and then we die. "When it is your time; it is your time."

I felt lucky to have gotten that from her.

After blaming God. I knew that was not the way to go. But everything I believed in before, didn't matter anymore.

I know God is love, he has always been with me my entire life and helps me through everything. When I pray, he always answers.

He loves and protects us. I was not going to blame God. I pray to him all the time.

I believe we are here to learn lessons.

But now, I needed to know more. It's too tough being on this earth without Kevin. I know he isn't coming back.

I started searching and searching. I needed answers that I could understand and accept.

I have so many questions.

I thought, why can't I communicate with my son? If mediums or psychics can communicate with loved ones on the other side, why can't I?

I joined two spiritual groups, which I do enjoy, and they do help me.

I checked out 15 different books from the library and read all the time.

I buried myself in reading, trying to find answers. I read books about losing a child. I read books on how to communicate with loved ones on the other side and many more.

I am not good with words and writing but I also started journaling and documenting this painful journey. It kept my mind occupied. I watched documentaries about the afterlife. I watched YouTube videos and also visited some mediums.

I was gripped with the desire to communicate with my son. I was determined to find out how I could.

I want to know what he is doing over there and what is the other side all about.

The more I read and searched for the truth, my perspective changed, which gave me a feeling of comfort and hope.

When you lose a child, there are so many things that you don't want to understand or accept.

I searched and searched and didn't want to believe anything I found.

Even though my loved ones surrounded me, all I could think about was the one that I had lost. They say I'll see him again when I die. That doesn't help me now. What about in the meantime?

Holidays came, and I try to make new traditions because the old ones just don't fit anymore. Nothing is the same ever again.

No matter how much I try to figure out why he died, it all comes down to "when it's your time, it's your time," Just like my mother said to me.

I was open-minded about the other side. I needed to find out more.

In my search, I learned a lot of things I had not really paid attention to before he died.

I started paying attention to the signs.

CHAPTER 4

THE SIGNS

The signs are everywhere. They help ease your grief. You may not realize that there was a sign until the event has passed. Just remember, there is no such thing as a coincidence.

Keep your eyes open you don't want to miss a thing.

Here are some of my signs.

My grief rushes through me to this day. It's a grief that surpasses all understanding unless you have lost a child. I pray that no one ever has to feel the hurt of this pain.

I will always grieve for my son. I will always wish he was here with me every day. I will always miss him.

As I go through the loss of his physical body, unable to touch him or hug him or kiss him. Not being able to watch Him fall in love and become a father and missing out on all his successes that were to come.

As much as I feel like I'm missing out. I can say without any doubt that my son was needed and that's why he was called back home.

I know I will see him again. I know this because of the signs I receive from my son, God, and my guardian angels. These dreams and signs that I have been blessed with and that continue to happen to me are what comforts me.

My eyes have been opened.

Always look for the signs.

SEVERAL DAYS LATER

The day of the Memorial Arrangements, my son Connor finally arrived home.

We had an appointment at the church to discuss how we were going to do the services.

We came home to talk to Connor about the services.

Music was playing in the background as I was telling him what was going on; Connor said, mom listen to what's playing on the radio right now.

The song was

"Only the good die young."

Several days later, we had an appointment at the funeral home at 10:00 am.

We left our house in plenty of time to get there. On the way, we made a wrong turn that took us through the cemetery. When we finally arrived late, Connor said, "Mom, look at the clock. It's 10:16.

That's Kevin's birthday." That was no coincidence.

As we were leaving the funeral home, Connor said, "Look at that tombstone. "It said Dick Swivel on it". That was such a brother like thing to point out.

I knew then that they would have both laughed at that name, had they seen it together. All three of us laughed.

We needed to eat. So, we decided to go get a Big Mac, because Kevin loved them. Another song came to us as we were leaving McDonald's and the singer was singing a song about, *"I'm all around you."*

It resonated very much with David and Connor. We had a brief moment of comfort.

Connor started working on his eulogy for the service.

The eulogy that he was writing was nice, although some of it was not appropriate. You know how brothers are. He read it to me again the night before the service.

On the day of the service, he stood up there at that podium and read the most beautiful unbelievable eulogy (Which you all read in chapter 2) It was not what he read to me the night before.

He read it with a sparkle in his

eyes and a smile on his face. It was obvious that he *is* a very proud of and loves his brother with all of his heart.

He said to me that Kevin came to him that night and they stayed up and wrote that eulogy together.

Kevin gave him the strength to be able to provide the eulogy as Connor wanted nothing more than for everyone to know Kevin the way he did for 25 loving years.

As I was getting ready for the service that morning a song came on. "Kiss and say goodbye. "The lyrics struck me. In short, they go like this:

This has got to be the saddest day of my life. I called you here today for a bit of bad news. I will not be able to see you anymore because of my obligations and the ties that you have.

That was a sign from Kevin.

I love you Kevin, forever and always.

MAY 4TH 2019

One week before Mother's Day.

I was feeling very sad. We had friends over visiting. They were concerned for us and interested in the signs I have been receiving. I ran upstairs to grab a book to show my friend—a book called "Life on the Other Side."

I opened the drawer on my nightstand to grab the book. Sitting right there on top were two Mother's Day cards from my boys they had given to me in middle school.

I got so excited I grabbed the cards and ran down the steps shouting, "Here is another sign!!!" It instantly filled my heart and gave me shivers! I know Kevin is here. I felt like my son did not forget me on Mother's Day. He made sure I went into that drawer and found those cards.

I got to experience the feeling of knowing, he is with me.

They were shocked and happy to be a witness to it. I left the cards on the counter so that I could have them on Mother's Day.

"Happy Mother's Day to me."

08/03/2019

This morning, Connor and I woke up to fly to San Francisco. Connor wanted to take me on a little weekend trip. It was a wonderful day. Now that it is getting closer to the evening, Connor and I were sitting on a concrete wall by the beach. You could see the Golden Gate Bridge and Alcatraz. It was very peaceful though we both had a moment. I mentioned to Connor, "We have not gotten any signs from Kevin all day. I thought for sure he was coming with us." Connor felt the same way.

We decided to take an Uber to Haight-Asbury Street, which is where a lot of Hippies hung out in the 60s. We walked all around having fun in the shops. Surrounded by all the beautiful artwork on the buildings and everywhere you look. We even went to see Jimi Hendrix's house. Kevin has a big picture of him on his bedroom wall.

As crowded as the streets were, a guy walked past Connor wearing a t-shirt from Kevin's first music festival.

A small town in Pennsylvania. It said 'Camp Bisco 2017.' What are the chances that someone would walk by us on a crowded street in San Francisco with a t-shirt from a small town in PA that happened to be Kevin's first music festival?

Slim to none.

He was with us.

We walked across the street to go into one of the little shops that had tie-dye clothing. All around us, music was playing. As we were walking out, Connor said, "Stop, mom listen to this song. I heard. *"Here I am baby signed, sealed, delivered. I'm yours,"* Connor pulled out his phone and showed me a text message he received from Kevin the day before he died, saying he loves this song. The signs are amazing. They come signed, sealed, and delivered. He is with us! We love you Kevin and thank you.

SPOTTING CARDINALS
SUMMER OF 2019

I never paid attention to the cardinals before, but now, I am seeing them all the time sitting on my fence or just flying around.

My sister-in-law was now experiencing them with me while we were lying out by the pool. She mentioned to me she thought they meant something spiritual. I also thought that too. So, we googled it and found this:

If you are lucky enough to spot a cardinal, you should smile to yourself as Cardinals represent deceased loved ones who are watching over you.

According to superstition, if you see a cardinal, one of your loved ones wants you to know that they're watching over you and that you are not alone.

I am lucky, and I am not alone.
Now I see signs all the time.

IN-NATURE DRAGONFLIES
SUMMERTIME 2019

A friend of mine came over to spend the day with me. She and I were sitting in the pool. We were chatting about this and that, and then she asked me how I was doing?

I started telling her about all the signs I've been receiving. At that moment, what felt like a bug flying all around me. She said to me, "That's a dragonfly." It was staying very close to me. It didn't go near her, only me. It was circling around me. I pointed my finger up to the sky and said, "Kevin is that you?"

The dragonfly then landed on the tip of my pointer finger and fluttered there. That freaked my friend out for a moment.

Now she, too, was seeing and experiencing the signs I am receiving.
I found out what a dragonfly symbolizes.

Dragonflies are spirit animals that symbolize new beginnings. Dragonflies in death are seen as spiritual representations that one's soul has been transformed and reborn.

God answered for me. He knows how deep my pain is. I am learning to adapt to this new life in a new way.

There were no words that I needed to say or speak the hurt is too painful to put into words. God knew that.

10/12/2019
KEVIN'S BIRTHDAY IN COLORADO

My brother, my sister in-law and I flew to Colorado to be with my son Connor to celebrate Kevin's birthday.

This was the first birthday we would be celebrating without him. He would have turned 28 years old.

We planned a wonderful trip to do all the things Kevin loved.

The first stop of the trip was us driving to all the little, small towns outside the city. We were all getting a good tour of the city as Connor drove us around. We ended up on our way to Black Hawk Casino and stopped for a bite to eat. Music was playing in the background while we waited to be seated.

As soon as we sat down, suddenly, A new song came on.

"Here I am baby, Signed Sealed Delivered I'm yours".

This is a song we hear from Kevin since that day in San Francisco.

I knew then he was with us, and we were going to have a magical weekend.

We did all the things Kevin would have loved. We went to the Tennessee Titans football game, which is Kevin's favorite football team they were playing in Denver on his birthday weekend.

Not a coincidence.

Then of course there was more surprises...

We also went to WWE Monday Night Raw a worldwide wrestling match that came to Denver that same weekend.

Lastly, we went to an amusement park in the city. They had three haunted houses for us to visit not just one but three. It was a tradition for us all to go to haunted houses on Kevin's birthday. We all loved the Halloween season as it was always connected to Kevin who made it that much more special.

After this weekend all I could say was "Wow unbelievable !!!!!"

We even visited the Red Rock amphitheater.

We did this all for you Kevin.
We had an amazing weekend full of fun and laughter.
Happy Birthday to my sweet child!!!

Thank you, Charlie and Connie, for being here for Connor and me on Kevin's weekend birthday.
Words cannot express how much you two mean to us.
You made a bigger impact than you realize.
I'll never forget your support, generosity, kindness and love.
We love you very much.

12/03/2019

I was in my home office paying bills. I had My TV on, in the background, with a music channel playing. I came across Kevin's credit card accounts. I started having a meltdown thinking about Kevin. Before this, I was crying and not having a good day. I miss him so much. I was crying so hard. Then suddenly, the music stopped playing on the TV.

I had Christmas music on, and then everything got quiet, and I heard a noise. Stella heard it too, she growled for a second. I went into the family room to see what happened. The cable box and the TV were both still on, but nothing was playing. I turned everything off and on again. Still nothing. I did it 3 times and then everything came back on. That was weird. It did stop me from crying, though.

Was that you Kevin? I love you, and I miss you, and thank you for the distraction you gave me. Thank you for all the signs you give me. Keep giving me every sign and please keep coming to me. I am always here for you. I love you.

01/12/2020

Connor came home for the weekend to watch the 2019 Super Bowl playoffs with us. The Titans finally made it to the playoffs. They were playing the Ravens, who were the number one team. The Titans were the underdog, and they were winning.

Kevin's friends came over also to watch with us.

At the end of the weekend, on the way to bringing Connor to the airport we stopped at my brother's house to have lunch with his family. I told them about the signs I been having. They were all very much enjoying my story. My brother is not a believer in signs or the supernatural. He just listened with a smile. We all got something to eat and were sitting around the kitchen table together talking.

Charlie was telling us that he's been cleaning out old boxes down in his basement all week, and he found this purse that belongs to his daughter Jacquie from when she was in middle school.

She's 36 now. He thought that she might want it since it's back in style again.

A camouflage Kate Spade purse. She was kind of excited to see it again, but she said no, she didn't want it. He said, well, throw it away. He didn't want it either. She went to the trashcan to throw it out and then, hesitated.

She said maybe I'll look at it again and then she put it back on the table.

Meanwhile, her sister Stefani arrived. Charlie wanted to play a joke on her.

He told her he bought her a new purse. She said I know the story behind this, with a laugh.

At that time Jacquie decided to pick up the purse to look through it.

Inside the purse, she saw a yellow post-it note folded up.

My husband said to her, oh what is that a love note from one of your boyfriends, ha-ha?

Then everyone started laughing.

She got this look of shock and disbelief on her face. She said you're not going to believe this. She showed us what was on the post-note.

KEVIN

Kevin's name was written on that yellow post-it note. We all were silent for a moment. I got chills and everyone couldn't believe what we just witnessed.

My brother called me the next day, still in shock. He couldn't believe what he had experienced.

I think he might be on his way to becoming a believer. Lol.

Nobody could explain how that happened. But I could, it was a sign from Kevin that he is all-around us and here for us all the time. Kevin loves his family so much, and he has not left us at all. We love you Kevin, so much. Keep the signs coming.

We love them all.

03/07/2020

It has been 1 year since Kevin's passing. The day we were dreading.

David and I got up and we just moped and cried all morning. We were not motivated to do anything but cry. Then David decided to turn the TV on.

He was surprised to see that the Caps (hockey) were playing the penguins. Kevin was a big hockey fan, and he loved the Caps. Out of all the teams that play together. Kevin especially liked when the Caps played the Penguins.

David said, I know what I'm doing. So, he ended up watching the game, and the Caps won. Yahoo!!

He went through the channels and found a station that was having a marathon on The Rolling Stones.

One of Kevin's favorite bands.

He also was checking other stations and there was a movie coming on later that evening called yesterday, which is about the Beatles.

Well, you guessed it, another one of Kevin's favorites.

David looked at me and said, this is a sign from Kevin. I said yes, he has the whole day planned out for you to enjoy.

I believe in signs.

Connor tells me he went into a brewery in the city to have a beer. He finished his beer; this is what was on the bottom of his Glass. The letter "**K** "

There's your sign.
Signs are everywhere,
you just need to believe.

08/13/2020
I SAW A "K" IN THE CLOUDS

Thinking about Kevin all day and shed some tears off and on.

David came home from work,
just by looking at me, he knew I
had been crying and I was very sad.

He said, "Let's go outside by the
pool and hang out for a little bit."
So, we did. We grabbed some beers, turned on the music, sat at
the table and played some cards
That was helping me to relax.

Then I decided to go lay
down on the lounge chair to listen
and watch the water flowing from
my cascade into the pool, that always
calms me down.

I started looking at the clouds and remembering last year I
saw Kevin's face in the clouds. Feeling kind of down, not really pay-
ing attention.

I saw a **K** formed in the clouds.
So, I was just thinking, oh, that looks like a K, and the first thing
that came to my mind was my Maiden name Karadimos.

It was like a light bulb went off inside my head that said, are you
crazy? Melodi (**K**) KEVIN.
Here is your sign!!!

I got so excited; I chuckled as it brought a big smile to my face.

Here I was drowning in my own sorrows that I almost missed a wonderful gift, a sign from my son. I told my husband and then we both started looking at the clouds together.

But nothing we saw beat the big **K.**

10/29/2020

I was lying in my bed thinking of
Kevin and I was talking to him.

Then I proceeded to get up, get
dressed and get my day started.

I went into his room to look around
and to feel closer to him.
I heard a soft noise when I walked
out of the room.

A feeling came over me, so I walked
back into Kevin's room and I saw
one of his pictures of himself fell
and landed face up with his beautiful
smile looking up at me.

I picked up the picture, sat down on his bed,
and looked at it and started talking to
him.
It made me so happy because I
knew that was a sign from Kevin.

He is letting me know everything is
going to be ok, and he is right here
by my side.

As I'm sitting there, I heard a ding
alerting me that I got a text message.
You're not going to believe who it was.
It was my other son Connor.
Who text me this message.

I love you forever and ever

Both of my boys were thinking of
me at the same moment.
I love my boys and how they are so
much in tune with each other.

Today it's a rainy day but it's
a sunny good day for me.

CONNOR'S SIGNS

My son Connor is a believer. He has experienced his own beautiful and
loving signs from his Big Brother Kevin. These stories are in his own
words as he shares with you some of the magical and tough moments
he has had since Kevin's passing…

03/08/2019

I woke up to a call from my mom's number very early in the morning.
It was my dad. He said he needed to tell me something – he said Kevin
passed away and you need to come home.

I fell to the ground. I try not to remember the immense feeling of pain, however alongside that pain I felt something I have never felt before. I had this Godly, spiritual, feeling of liberation, a rush of energy picked me up from the ground – it was Kevin, I looked out my window with brand new eyes. I could see and feel what seemed like my life flashing before me. Yes, this feeling was short lived, but in that brief moment I caught a glimpse of the future and felt what was just enough to give me strength to pull it together.

This was and will be the worst day of my life. I needed to get home quick. The same day a few hours later I had to hop on an airplane for 4 hours. I sat there in the aisle seat crying with this heavy weight bearing over me, I am so heartbroken. I remember having to tell the flight attendant what happened as I was probably making people uncomfortable as I sat and cried for hours. I will never forget the look on her face as she cried with me. She showed compassion in that moment which I really needed. I don't know how I survived that plane ride from Hell. I was so confused; I had no idea how this happened. He was supposed to move out here with me.

What felt like an eternity – the plane finally landed. I ran off as fast as I could called my Mom and Dad and then found them at the pickup line. I jumped in the car and we all just let it out. We took turns being there for one another. I was never more relieved to see my family but now what crushed me was this was the new family minus Kevin. I couldn't process any thoughts. My reality was destroyed. Nothing felt real. Any other death, just knowing if I had Kevin, I felt I could survive. He is my other half. Without him I began to feel lost.

03/13/2019

Today was a really quiet and sad day. The thing about death is people around you start to get back to their daily lives, but the ones closest don't know how too. This was one of those days. I knew I couldn't sleep as the night began to approach so I was on the couch just crying with my family. My Dad said he was going to head upstairs and try to get some rest. I got up off the couch walked over to him gave him and hug and I said "I love you dad" -and before he could say anything back the TV Commercial immediately goes "I love you Dad".

We all heard it – the exact moment I said I love you dad, the TV says it too. Only that it wasn't just the TV, it was Kevin! We always told our mom and dad we love them. Once one of us said it the other immediately would say it too. This was amazing and no coincidence. I believe. Thank you, Kevin.

3/22/2019

Every day before getting up and going to work I struggled, but the world is still turning, and I had priorities. As much as I wanted to lay in bed, I had to go in. My first call of the day at work was for a role in Dublin, OH. I had a nice lady named Susan apply who I planned on giving a call. I pulled up her resume and started dialing I noticed on the 2nd page she helped out a restaurant owner in my home town, WV. I was like huh what a "coincidence" – only for this conversation to be so amazing and truly unworldly.

The lady answers. I told her why I was calling and that she had applied for a role in Dublin, OH. She began to go over her reason for applying and we chatted for a few minutes about her recent experience. Then it was my moment to bring up Martinsburg, WV! I said to her I saw Martinsburg on your resume, and I am from Martinsburg (even though I'm calling from Colorado) She began to tell me how she loves Martinsburg and was helping her daughter at a restaurant called Habanero.

My heart sunk to the floor…Kevin worked at Habanero back while he was in school. I told her that my brother worked there before. She goes "Who is your brother" I said "Kevin Shipley" – she goes OMG I love Kevin. He is so funny and one of a kind. This is such a small world.

She asked me how he was doing and I not wanting to talk about it said good. He is doing good.

After our call. I really couldn't believe how here I am in Colorado, calling for a role in Ohio and I somehow find somebody who worked at one point in my hometown and knows my brother Kevin.

About 20 minutes later I receive a call again from Susan She didn't seem as bubbly when I first talked to her and said she called her daughter to tell her she met Kevin's brother and heard some news…I told her that it was true. She shared a moment with me on the phone, she expressed again how much of an amazing man Kevin was. He is so loved. Everywhere he went he had an impact on people.

This made my day and I believe in you dear lord. The universe has so much magic behind it and the more I feel you believe the more you will see. Though signs bring comfort they don't bring back Kevin who I miss every day.

4/8/2019

I have been back to work for a few weeks now. I don't feel normal, but the distraction helps.

I had a small conversation with a coworker.

She told me her brother had died when she was in school.

I never knew this, and I told her how sorry I was to hear that, and we both expressed our emotions towards our brothers.

She said her parents still celebrate every birthday. I asked her politely when that was – she said her brothers birthday is October 16th.

I was speechless.

That is also Kevin's birthday.

I told her and the look of her face…we both got chills. This was a healing conversation and a 1/365 chance of sharing the same birthday.

I don't believe in coincidences anymore. I love you Kevin and may her brother also rest in peace.

9/14/2019

I booked a flight to LA to clear my head for the weekend.

One thing I had noticed in my healing journey was that there is something special about traveling and being on the go.

Every time I was in a different city, I was seeing something new. I would see people, places, and feel a sense of something more and bigger to life

I sometimes would think each and every one of these folks has their own story. Some of them are probably going through grief just like me.

As soon as I got off the airplane, I was a bit nervous. I had been to LA before but this time I had planned on driving a car. I was excited for the weekend, but at this stage in my life excitement is kind of bland. Grief likes to sneak up on you when you're happy and try to remind you why you shouldn't be.

This was starting to happen to me. I went to the car rental place and got in my car. I said a brief prayer, I took a deep breath and pressed the start engine. As I was driving out, the employee said before I left, he needed the paperwork on the top of the dashboard.

I reached over to grab it and on the piece of paper it said, this vehicle was "serviced by Kevin". Wow!

Kevin had looked over my vehicle, made sure it was safe to use and now it was time to get my weekend started. I was in the right moment and right state of mind to be aware and soak in this beautiful sign.

I had such an amazing trip and it started off knowing I am in the right place, I am present in the moment, and I am aware. Thank you for this wonderful sign and reassurance. I love you

03/13/2020

For the last couple of months, I have heard that on Friday the 13th, local tattoo shops in the area do specials. This one happened to be in March 2020 so 1 year after Kevin's death.

I was excited and knew I had to get one.

I found a cool shop right up the street from my house.

Overall, my whole day was fun. I saw a few designs that resonated with me before and then the energy of it being Friday the 13th in the air was really cool.

The tattoo ended up turning out great; my "special" edits were also put on.

These little edits made the tattoo more personal for me.

The tattoo held strong meaning to me and Kevin's sacred bond. As I got up from the table and went to put my shoes on, I went over to a chair and sat down.

I exhaled, reached down and as I grabbed my shoe, I looked up and saw a huge box on the floor that said (brother at your side).

This was the Brother printer and the box was in bright letters saying Brother at Your Side.

Crazy! I felt this rush of love and powerful energy run through my body.

I knew Kevin was there, and I was supposed to get this tattoo. These moments help me carry on knowing there is a bigger picture.

03/4/2021
HAPPY BIRTHDAY

I went to Miami Beach, Florida to celebrate my birthday. It really sucks having a birthday 3 days before the anniversary of your brothers passing. It doesn't make you want to celebrate. There are times when you don't want to, but you must. I love myself so I treated myself.

I wasn't going to let anything stop me from having a good time.

I rented a convertible and was driving around in the Florida sunshine. I felt free and relaxed. I was listening to Sirius radio and enjoying the music. The station had been advertising a call-in contest over the radio.

Then here is where my one-of-a-kind sign came.

Between songs the DJ came on to announce the winner of an ongoing contest. He said we got a very special person here and were on the phone with today's winner Kevin.

The DJ was like "yoooo Kevin congrats man" and that's when Kevin goes "it's my birthday too!" They wished Kevin a happy birthday and proceeded to play the jams. This was my brother wishing me a happy birthday.

Kevin, you will always be our winner.

I love you.

05/25/21
DMV TRIP

The DMV's had been closed because of the pandemic so I was still driving on temporary tags. When I say they expired, I mean they were really expired. I was certainly not motivated to go on a weekday before a long day's work to the DMV. Who really is though?

I got up at the crack of dawn in hopes to get there before it opened. I walked into my bathroom knowing this was about to be a LONG day. I said a prayer. I said, "Dear God, Dear Kevin, please give me a sign and the strength to make it through this day".

I had arrived at the DMV, and I wasn't the only one with the idea of getting there before they opened. The line was out the door. I took my spot in line and began to wait.

I got closer to the door and that is when this elderly lady started walking up from her car. She was not in line with the rest of us who had been standing for 30+ minutes. She was definitely doing the "I'm a poor old lady who doesn't see the line". She cut in front of us all. I saw a few people look and the guy behind her said "excuse me", but nobody did anything. I started laughing to myself as I knew exactly what she did. Soon after I had forgot about it as there is no reason to be angry, I told myself.

Finally, I had got inside the DMV. I was given a ticket and told to take a seat. A few minutes passed and I saw the old lady getting helped. I laughed again and said to myself man she really played it well as now she's almost done.

Now it's my turn. I go up to the counter and tell the lady I am here to get my tags as I have expired ones. She asked for the paperwork which always gives you a mini heart attack, thinking I know I have everything but do I? Well, I had everything. She turns around in her seat, pulls out from the drawer a license plate and puts it on the counter. There it was…my sign.

Thank you to the lady who cut in line.

Thank you, God and Kevin, for giving me the strength to finally accomplish this task as now I sit here with one of the greatest signs I have received.

I walked out of the DMV with my plates in hand and I see it loud and clear the first 3 letters of my plate are BRO.

We are forever BRO's

There was my sign. I had received custom plates from God and Kevin.

Kevin you are my only brother, my best friend, and my angel. I miss you every day, but these signs let me know I will see you again.

CHAPTER 5

IN DREAMS

I started having dreams of Kevin,
which I found out later are called visitations.
When you have these dreams, they are your loved ones visiting you.
They can leave you messages or just talk to you.
The best dreams ever.

04/6/2019
FIRST DREAM
4:30 AM

I woke up to a ding from my cell phone.

It was my niece texting me about the birth of her fourth grandchild.

I fell back into a deep sleep.

Before I knew it, I was having my first dream of Kevin. He appeared in front of me.

He had short hair.

No mustache or beard; his face was clean shaven and clear.

He was wearing a white tank top with his yellow swim trunks.

Behind him was a glow that looked like sunshine and lights.

Upon seeing him, I felt peaceful and calm.

He looked so handsome.

I asked him what had happened to him, a couple of times.

He said he fell in and out of sleep.

Then he disappeared.

04/8/2019
2ND DREAM

Two days later.

I couldn't sleep. I got in bed at 11:00 pm. The next day was going to be the first day I would be home by myself.

David had to go back to work.

After hours of restlessness, I finally fell into a deep sleep.

In that dream I saw Kevin again.

He looks so happy.

I couldn't stop staring and looking at him. I felt a tremendous amount of love. It all felt so real.

I said, Kevin, I want you here with me

He said, "Oh Mom. I'm happy here." Then he disappeared from my dream.

My eyes stared opening up and that's when I saw a full-body spirit of Kevin gliding away from my bed, heading towards the door with his head hanging down. He didn't look back to see if I saw him, he just glided away.

He had a maroon T-shirt on with black running shorts and his compression tights underneath.

It may have started as a dream, but with my eyes, I saw him gliding away. I am awake, and it is 3 am.

I felt that he was in my dreams and also standing by my bed watching over me in spirit.

This is all new to me right now, so much to take in. I'm ready for this JOURNEY!!!!!

Thank you, Dear God.

JUNE 2019
3RD DREAM

Kevin is coming to me in my dreams. I'm enjoying this. He looked content. It felt so real seeing him again. I started asking him a lot of questions, and he was answering them, but for some reason, I kept on forgetting what I was asking him and what his answers were. I said, in my thoughts "Dear God, please let me remember some of the questions and answers. So, God gave me two questions and answers to remember.

One of the questions that I remember was this, "I asked Kevin, "Everything that I believed in and told you about the other side is it true?

He shook his head yes.

2nd question, am I on the right path?
He shook his head and answer with a resounding "yes".
That made me feel good, that I'm on the right path.

He said Mom, it was just my time. I had to go.

There are no answers that will ever make sense when you lose a loved one.

The only thing that matters is when it's your time, it's your time. You *can't* stop it.

09/22/2019

In the early morning after 7 am, I fell back into a deep sleep. I began to dream. I saw Kevin walking around the football/baseball field.

He had his Titans beanie hat on with his favorite white, light blue and dark blue jacket. The same outfit he wore when we were in Colorado.

I moved closer to him.

In my thoughts (we didn't speak any words) I said I want to hug you and he gave me a big hug and I felt it.

It was amazing. I truly felt his real-life earthly hug.

I knew that his hug was real, and I thanked him in my dreams for hugging me.

I finally felt him still close to me.

I have been praying and praying to God, Kevin and my angels to come into my dreams and for me to feel him. My prayers were answered. I felt him.

Thank you
Kevin, I love you.

12/11/2019

I woke up around 3:00 am. Every night I'm looking into Kevin's room, trying to see him. I fell back to sleep and started dreaming that Kevin was six years old.

I was holding onto Kevin at the hospital because he was going into surgery. They said he might not make it. I thought to myself, oh no am I going to lose him again, he already died. I held on to him tight I didn't want to let go. He was laughing and smiling, and I was just holding onto my baby.

I enjoyed seeing Kevin as my little boy once again.

What a crazy dream, or was this a visitation?

02/15/2020

It was 6 am, when I woke up.

I closed my eyes to meditate and go back to sleep. As I close my eyes, I started seeing red and orange colors, they were blending together.

There also was an opening from the clouds where I saw blue skies. Then my son Connor appeared, sudden, Kevin appeared also, right behind and above Connor with a bright light shining and a huge smile on his face.

The impression I got, was Kevin showing me that he's protecting and watching over him.

Thank you, Kevin, for being Connors's big brother.

I love you.

02/17/2020

I took Stella, Kevin's dog, out for a walk. When I came back home, I went upstairs to lay down. I fell into a deep sleep and started dreaming that David and I moved back to our old house in Columbia, MD.

I loved my old house. It's where

David and I created our family. We lived on a cozy cul-de-sac, perfect for our boys, our first home.

We were sitting in the living room and Michelle was visiting us.

I said to my husband, "Why did we move back here?

He said, "I thought you wanted to come back?

I said, but there's nobody here anymore.

It was true, my brother and sister-in-law lived right around the corner, but they moved. All our friends that lived there had all left.

I walked towards the front door to open it and look outside.

And that's when I saw this little boy, maybe 4 or 5 years old, sitting out there in the grass by the mailbox and driveway.

He had his knees pulled up and his hands around his knees, his head was facing down to the ground.

That little boy looked so heartbroken.

There was nobody else out there playing in the cul-de-sac.

He was all by himself, very lonely just sitting there.

As I remembered, kids were always outside playing there,
it was a happy site to see.
But this time it was gloomy and sad.

I woke up out of that dream very emotional.

I sat there and thought about the dream and started sobbing uncontrollable.

In my dream, when I opened the front door and saw that little boy by himself, it broke my heart.

I felt that he was Connor.

He was without his brother, who always was there with him, playing and being by his Side.

There should've been two little boys sitting out front. But instead, there was only one lonely little boy who misses his only brother very much.

This is how I interpreted the dream, that the past is the past and nothing can be changed. If we went back in time, Kevin would have still died, no matter what. No one can change that outcome.

Because your death is already pre-planned, we chose that before we come down here.

When it's your time it's your time.

I need to start moving forward, living and making a new life on this earth without Kevin. And that's the problem, how can I do that?

I can't, that's why I'm trying to communicate with the other side.

We miss you so much Kevin.

We need you.

I'm never going to stop trying to find ways to see and communicate with you.

Our love is too strong, and it will never break. I am with you always and I know you are always with me.

I love you forever.

03/15/2020

Another dream, I was in a big picnic area with many people all around.

Stella was running everywhere

Connor and my sister-in-law were with me, and my brother was in the car talking to David who was very upset.

My brother was comforting him.

They got out of the car and was coming towards us.

As they got closer, I saw Kevin standing right next to his father, walking with him side-by-side.

I got so excited. I asked Connor, "Do you see your brother?"

There are no words to describe the look on Connor's face when he said, "Yes," while shaking his head up and down, filled with happiness and shock.

David went over to sit by Connor, and Kevin follow him and stay right by his side. He sat there with them. All three together again.

I now know that Kevin is watching over his father and protecting him. That's what I felt Kevin wanted me to know in this dream.

Daddy protected his two boys, and now Kevin is doing the same thing.

What a dream!!!

03/19/2020

A friend in one of my spiritual groups gave me a pendulum.

She told me how to use it and that it's used for yes and no answers. I have been using the pendulum; it is very interesting.

I asked the pendulum if I was going to see Kevin tonight.

It gave me the symbol for yes.

I went upstairs to go to bed. I looked into Kevin's room and didn't see anything. I laid in bed, I closed my eyes and fell right to sleep. During the night, I woke up and looked into Kevin's room. I saw nothing. Yes, I am searching for him.

I fell back to sleep.

I woke up, off and on, during the whole night looking.

At 7 am, I woke up again then went back into a deep sleep.

There it was I had a beautiful dream.

I was standing in my kitchen. My boys were in the living room playing Nintendo and talking to each other having the time of their life.

My boys were back together again. It was the most wonderful feeling.

It felt so real I went over to Kevin; I was just hugging and kissing all over him.

Telling him how much I love him and miss him, and I was so glad he came into my dream.

He just looked and smiled and then hugged me back.

All of a sudden, I heard a door open that woke me up, and I couldn't get my dream back.

But it left me with a great feeling inside that I got to see him again. I like my pendulum, it said Yes!!!

I was lying in bed. Before I knew it, I fell asleep and started dreaming. I was with three girlfriends, we were hanging outside, the grass was green there were hills and flat areas.

People were all over the place, reminded me of a park.

Someone's phone was ringing off the hook. One of the girls said whose phone is ringing like that. I looked down to check my phone, and it was my phone going off!!!!

I had 23 missed calls, all from Kevin.

At that moment, I went into a panic attack. I knew something was wrong.

I started looking for him.

Then suddenly, I saw Kevin down the hill. He was standing outside by an old red phone booth. It was one of those Clark Kent (Superman) would change in.

He was wearing his blue full body wet suit.

The exact same wet suit that he had on when he died.

I got the feeling that something terrible has happened.

Then I saw that he was crying. This upset me tremendously. I started running down the hill as fast as I good.

I went into a panic mode, because I knew something terrible had happened. I wanted to get to him as fast as I good.

I tried calling him back.

Then I remembered in my dream that he had died.

I was so scared.

I woke up crying with tears flowing down my cheeks.

Is this a message? or just a dream?

More of a nightmare.

10/25/2020
5:15 AM

I saw my son in his room. I will discuss this in more detail in the next chapter about spirits.

I closed my eyes and went back to sleep and now I had a dream about Kevin visiting me.

We were together in a big space. I did not see any walls. There were spirits siting at theses tables eating and drinking it reminded me of a cafeteria. Kevin was naming all the things that he likes to eat and drink over there on the other side, but I can't remember what they were. We started gliding, just moving along. No effort of walking or running, just gliding. I asked him if he knew what my purpose now was in life,

because I always thought my purpose was raising my two boys he casually said, "write a book." It wasn't convincing, so I said, "Are you just saying that, or is that really my purpose? he said, "No, I'm not just saying that, it's your purpose."

I really can't remember much more than that, but I felt comfortable. He was very happy. It made me feel like he was at home there. He wasn't missing out on anything from earth. He's so handsome, relaxed, calm, and loving. Which he was all that here on earth. I guess things are just meant to be. We are only down here for a short amount of time.

JANUARY 2021
2 DREAMS OF KEVIN

Dream 1

I had my boys together again.

I was watching them hanging around like they always did.

There was a huge ski slope.

They both had their own inner tube.

They were tubing down these huge mountains

I knew I was dreaming, but it felt very real, like Kevin was here with me, I somehow knew God let him come down here to be with me for a while. I don't know for how long. All I knew is that I was extremely happy to see him.

I had my boys together again.

I was watching them hanging out like they always did.

Connor went first and made it to the end. He was laughing so hard.

Kevin jumped on his inner tube and was heading down the slope, he hit a bump. He flew high in the sky, and I mean high in the sky.

I thought, OMG he's going to die again.

He came down and landed right on the inner tube and kept sliding down to the end and was laughing so hard.

That made me laugh.

Both of my boys laughing and having a great time with each other again. It felt so real and good. My mind couldn't believe he was here. That's how real it felt to my heart.

I was thanking God for giving him back to me again. I didn't let the "How long" get to me even though I want him to be here forever.

I was just enjoying every moment that I had with him at that time.

Dream 2

Kevin came to visit me again in my dreams.

He was hugging me, and I was kissing him.

I was so lucky that he was here with me again.

Everything is all so real even though I know that he's not here on earth, it feels like he is.

He looks real he feels real.

We're communicating. Yahoo!!

I don't know-how. It's all feelings.

We were looking at each other face-to-face.

I asked him did you meet Jesus? He shook his head up and down, Yes.

I said, "what about God."

He said," I heard God."

For some reason, I can't remember any more of that dream, but there was more.

SEEING KEVIN IN MY MEDITATIONS
6/2021

I can't remember what day it was in June, but I woke up, lying in my bed. I thought I would do some meditation.

I saw colors, and I was meditating for Kevin to come through. I haven't seen him for a while, and I love seeing him.

I was in a very relaxed meditation stage.

I saw red and green colors, then I saw a hand, and I knew it was Kevin's hand.

I saw his face come through in the red color.

Then as clear as day I was right there with Kevin.

He was sitting on the couch, and I was standing by the kitchen table just watching him, He was full of excitement with a big smile on his face.

He wanted to show me something he had that was little.

Not sure what it was at first, he's laughing with excitement, saying look what I got, and he put it down on the floor. I got so excited I didn't know what it was, and then I realized it was a little dog that looked like a younger version of Stella, his dog.

I enjoyed it, and it made me so happy that I had the next best thing about him being alive and seeing him in my meditation. It was like watching a movie from the projector.

Thank you, Kevin, for coming through. You never let me down; I love you, my son.

06/19/2021

I had a sweet dream of Kevin.

He was about ten years old. I was back in time. I loved every moment of it.

He came over to me and took my hand, and said, "Mommy let me show you something." We walked into a room which was his old bed room when he was a little boy back in our old house. I couldn't believe what I saw. It was exactly like his old room. He sat down on his bed and started reading his books. I was amazed at how everything was so clear and so real.

I felt like I was really there.

I knew I was dreaming, but I didn't want to wake up. I wanted to stay back in time.

CHAPTER 6

SPIRITS

I started seeing my son and other spirits.

I read that if you start seeing spirits do not be afraid. If you are afraid, they will not come back. when I saw my son for the first time, I made sure that I stayed calm and showed no fear. It was the most beautiful experience. God gave me the gift of Kevin for eternity whether it's here on earth or the other side.

In addition to my research and in my readings, I have found that between the hours 3am - 7am is when spirits of people who deeply love us come to visit because that is the time our minds are fully rested, receptive and are open to their messages. They **will** tap you or make a noise to wake you up. We are rested and in a better state of mind at that time. These are the teaching hours.

07/31/2019

Today I am flying out to visit Connor in Colorado. Then we are going to fly out and spend a day together in San Francisco.

I woke up at 5 AM. I had to take a double look. I wasn't sure what I was seeing. I blinked my eyes a couple times and then i realized I was seeing a spirit. There was a Spirit standing next to my bedroom door facing the wall in the hallway. She had short blonde hair to her shoulders, and it flipped up at the ends. She was wearing a white blouse with black pants.

As she was gliding by me, I realized that this was a spirit. I was shocked, scared, surprised, excited, all at the same time, just for an instant and then it quickly passed, I had to calm myself down. This is what I have been waiting for, now it's finally here.

I knew she was going to bring Kevin to me.

I looked at where she was looking and saw in a movie projection style parts of Kevin flashing like his eyes, his mouth, his mustache and beard. It appeared she was showing him or teaching him how to project himself on the wall. I kept looking harder and harder and then suddenly I saw a full body of Kevin on the wall in the hallway. He looked vibrant and handsome with a beautiful happy smile on his face. He was full of excitement and proud that his whole body came through. He did it! He accomplished it. He waved at me to make sure I saw him. I waved back and then he disappeared. I stared at the wall for a little bit, but I couldn't see anything more than a blank wall.

I was so overwhelmed and shocked.

I couldn't believe what I just saw, a spirit and my son. It was not a dream it was real. I sat up in my bed, then I reached over to the nightstand and picked up my phone to write this down and try to explain what I just saw.

A beautiful feeling came over me.

I knew from there on, I'm going to be able to see my son, even if it's for a split second.

I still can't explain the feeling that I had, it was like a spiritual light lit up my heart.

Now I'm ready to go visit my other son in Denver.

08/30/2019
ANGEL MAN

My niece, Michelle, and I were in Colorado visiting Connor.

Connor was working that first day, so we decided to explore downtown Denver. We walked along these little city streets, there-were musicians playing on corners, people walking all around, the wind was blowing with the warm sun shining bright. Kevin was on our minds. He always is. We had lunch and walked into a couple of shops. We got tempted to buy a little bag of donuts on the side of the street, so we bought two which were delicious. Connor texted me to let us know he got off work early and was heading home. So, we headed back towards the bus stop. We got on the bus to head home. Due to the Labor Day festival, they closed the streets, so the bus took us back to where we first got on. So, we got off the bus and started walking.

Our path changed.

Instead of going down the street where Connor lives, we went down the opposite street over. Our path home kept on changing.

As we were walking down the street Michelle and I got into a deep conversation about Kevin.

This time when she stopped in her tracks to tell me her thought, I noticed out of the corner of my eye a man walking towards us. I said to Michelle, "we need to keep walking, we're blocking the sidewalk." She turned around and we both said sorry to the man. The man continued walking across the grass to get in front of us. He said you all look like you were in a deep conversation. Michelle said, "oh well yes, we were." Then the man asked," do you mind if I ask you what you were talking about?"

Michelle and I looked at each other with a puzzled look then she said "no, we were just talking about if it's your time, is it your time? do you believe that?" he then shook his head and said "yes, I do." This caught our attention. Sweat was dripping down his face and he asked if we could move to the shade under the tree, so we moved, and he started talking and explaining things in a way that was the same as how we think and believe. We felt that he was wise and intelligent. He then proceeded to give us examples of whether it's your time or not.

He said, I can walk across that street and the car won't hit me. Michelle said "how do you know that?" He said "the car will stop because he sees me, or he will slam on his brakes or he would avoid me by swerving to the other side". "If it were my time the car would hit me, and I would die, because it's my time."

Michelle had a water bottle in her hand.

Then he said to her give me a sip of your water. Michelle said no I don't want germs and gave him the bottle anyway, he actually took a sip out of the water bottle.

He said my whole life I've never drank out of a stranger's water bottle. This time I decided to step out of the box and take a sip from a stranger's water bottle. If it was my time to go, I would've died because little did, I know the water had poison in it.

If it wasn't my time to die, I would've thrown up and gotten very sick. He continued to explain that when it's our time to die sometimes people will do things that they normally never do self-consciously. They consciously don't know this but it's their time to die. When it's our time it's our time.

I told him that my son recently passed away and that I'm having a hard time, I am looking for answers, comfort and closure. He said to me that it was his time. Then he asked us if he could say a prayer, we said yes. He put his hands out in front of us we put our hands-on top of his and he said the most beautiful prayer that I have ever heard in my entire life. His voice changed and became much deeper and his tone it sounded like nothing either of us had ever heard before. It sounded like it was orchestrated. It was indescribable. The rhythm and harmony in his voice was beautiful. It was fluid like water. I have never heard a priest, pastor or minister speak in such ways. The busy streets were no longer busy, and it felt as if we were frozen in time and only in the moment. He prayed to God for him to give me comfort and closure and to send me pennies to show that he is with me all the time. He acted like he knew all of us in this prayer because of all the beautiful things he said about us. When he described Kevin as a beautiful man, he made it sound like he has known him forever and still knows him and that he is on the other side.

After the prayer I said to Michelle," We have to go because Connor has been texting and waiting for us to get home. "As we said goodbye Michelle whisper to me, that man said, "See you soon." As we were walking away Michelle said who would say see you soon? He is a stranger why would we see him soon. Then Michelle said I think he is an angel.

I said let's turn around and see if he's still there.

We turned around. He was standing way back in the same place we left him standing there looking at us. I yelled are you an angel?

He reached his hands out from his sides and said

"I am who I am. "

Michelle and I just stood there as if time stopped. We were frozen and couldn't speak all we could do is wave back. In those moments we both knew without a doubt that he is an angel... I said to Michelle let's turn around again and see where he's at. He was gone nowhere in sight.

Wouldn't he have continued walking in the direction that he was originally headed. Behind us or with us? He didn't. He stood and watched us walk away.

After this experience I had many conversations with my niece about our encounter. There are a few more things that we like to add here about Angel Man. He had the darkest brown eyes that looked straight into our eyes as he talked. Black hair, a darker complexion. He looked like he could have been Greek, Jewish, or Italian?

He was carrying one of those metal/utility/ grocery carts that was broken. That has to mean

Something? But what?

He made me feel peaceful and calm which supplied a healing that lasted the whole weekend.

Thank you, dear God.

At that time, I did not know what was going on. Now I do know. God sent me Angel Man.

08/31/2019

The next day we went to the Denver festival downtown.

They had a free concert with KC and the Sunshine Band playing on the stage outside.

Everyone was gathering all-around we were close to the stage.

KC was talking in between singing songs, then out of nowhere he said

"Here I am baby Sign, Sealed,
Delivered. I'm yours"
Then proceeded to start singing a different song and dancing.
I was excepting him to sing that song.
I couldn't believe what I heard. I asked Connor did you hear what I heard.

He shook his head up and down.

I said what did you hear?

'Here I am baby Signed, Sealed, Delivered. I'm Yours'

I said Michelle did you hear that too she said Yes!!

WOW UNBELIEVABLE

Two days later while still in Colorado, we went to an Italian restaurant. I pulled out my chair and Connor pointed out that there was a penny under my chair (there's my sign) When I got home from my trip there was a penny inside of an empty suitcase that I brought back home with me.

Spirits, Pennies and Signs everywhere.

We love you Kevin and thank you again for sending us all these beautiful reminders that there is more around us than we ever know.

09/12/2019

Thursday morning around 5am I was in a deep sleep on the living room couch recovering from knee surgery, when I heard a voice whisper to me 'wake up." without hesitation I sat up immediately.

My eyes were drawn to the T.V. Screen.

I saw a reflection of the wall where Kevin's pictures hang. Quickly, I realized there was a spirit of a young woman with long brown hair who looked exactly like me.

She was standing by the same wall. Her voice is what woke me up. I stared at her, and thought is she my daughter and then she disappeared.

I immediately had this overwhelming feeling of love.

I pray that she comes back to visit me.

I don't control who I see, nor do I always understand the reasoning behind them. This woman resembled a younger me and I felt this strong sense of warmth and love.

10/24/2019
THE MAN IN THE MIRROR

I woke up at 3:58 am. I automatically sat up in my bed with my eyes focused directly at the mirror on my dresser. I saw the same blonde hair spirit that was with Kevin the first time. This time it wasn't the back of her head it was her face and body.

She was clapping and dancing with no sound. In her dance moves her arms were swaying and pointing to her right. I had this knowing that she was with Kevin. Out of nowhere he appeared in the mirror too. He was dancing and smiling. Then they both disappeared.

11/14/2019
KEVIN CAME TO ME

Tonight, I went to bed at 12:30 AM.

David left for work at 3 AM which woke me up. I fell back into a deep sleep, and I had a nightmare.

There was a man that was getting ready to kidnap me, so I started screaming help. It was loud enough that I woke myself up. As I was screaming at the top of my lungs, I saw a spirit coming towards me. It was a silhouette of Kevin's body. I said Kevin is that you? he shook his head yes. He was in his spiritual body.

He was wearing a maroon shirt and black gym shorts over top of his black compression pants. It was the exact same outfit that I saw him in my 2nd dream in Chapter 5.

He started floating backwards and moving away I said Kevin I'm not screaming at you I had a nightmare. Stay, please stay I'm not afraid of you. Don't go Kevin. I said again I'm not afraid of you, don't leave, please don't leave. He moved back behind my bedroom door. I stayed in bed and kept looking at the door and kept on talking to him to let him know that I'm not afraid I want to see him, I said, "please come out. I stayed staring at the door then I fell back to sleep. I turned over on my other side to sleep. On this side, by David's dresser, I saw a Spirit and I knew it was Kevin. He blended in with the dresser I kept looking and looking I said Kevin is that you, he waved his hand at me.

I stayed awake looking and waiting and I saw his face come through and then he would blend back in with the picture on the wall and his face would come out again and I could see his face and his body. I kept on talking to him telling him how much I love him and miss him and how I want nothing more than to see and communicate with him but there were no words from him, even so, I just kept on looking I couldn't take my eyes off of him. His face would peek through from time to time from behind the picture. I went back into a deep sleep and the most amazing thing happened to me. It was very real. Kevin was right there in my bed.

He just hugged me and hugged me and hugged me and I hugged him back I didn't what to let go.

He felt human to me, not a spirit.

I said oh my Dear God, you have given me Kevin back. For a moment I really thought he did,

that's how real it felt.

He just had this cheerful happy smile and glow to him.

Normally he comes and goes so quickly. This time it felt like forever.

The hug, the feeling, he filled my heart up with love. We held each other like there was no tomorrow. I finally felt peaceful that I saw him for real.

He was with me. He always would jump in my bed when I was laying in the bed and hug me and that's exactly what he did. Just as if he never died. I love you Kevin with all my heart. Thank you for giving me this wonderful memory to treasure. I love all the signs and I love seeing your spirit. Please keep it up you're doing a great job on the other side. We are so proud of you we've always been and always will be. I felt like he was alive for a moment. I had my son back and it felt incredible. I love you Kevin and I'm always here for you.

11/17/2019
THE BOW

I was laying in my bed looking towards Kevin's room.

I saw Kevin in his room laying on his bed and I saw his face. I had to look hard and concentrate. He comes and goes. I saw his face again, one minute he's there the next minute he's gone. This time-when I saw him, he looked at me. I waved to him. He waved back and then he disappeared. I laid there for a while looking to see if I could see him again and fell into a deep sleep.

At 8:18am the dog started barking which woke me up. I saw a ball of white light in Kevin's room. The light started changing shape and tying itself into a bow and landed where the wall meets the ceiling at the corner of his window then it unraveled itself into a straight white line of light and shot straight up like a lightning bolt through the ceiling and disappeared.

Very strange, what does this mean?

Michelle interprets that the bow represents a Gift, and she believes that the gift is for me.

After this I closed my eyes and started seeing red and black colors. I saw my sons face through the red color. He was trying to write something, but I couldn't read it. There were words he was writing in cursive, but they kept disappearing too quickly.

As fast as he wrote the words, they disappeared. It was so fast. It looked like scribbling. I couldn't understand one letter. I opened and closed my eyes real fast. I saw the same thing again. He was writing things and crossing out words and writing again. I opened and closed my eyes again. I still could not read it. I know he is trying to send me a message but this time I couldn't quite get it. There were no vowels in the writing. It appeared in a cursive scribble.

I love you Kevin please keep trying I'll always be here for you.

11/19/2019

I woke up at 4:43 am. I saw Kevin and he was with a different blonde-haired girl this time.

They were standing next to each other.

They saw me and both started waving. I got so excited, and I waved back. They both glided up out of his bedroom above the stairway banister next to his bedroom door.

Kevin was beaming with his amazing smile. He looked so happy. She was beautiful and she looked so happy too. They both had a glorious glow to them. As I was looking at them Kevin started to point at his toes. He had no shoes on. They started dancing with each other right in the air.

He twirled her around and picked her up over his head. It was exciting. I was extremely surprised seeing him and watching him. I never knew that my son could dance so gracefully. It was something that you would see on Dancing with the Stars. It was that magical.

I asked him who is that blonde hair girl. She then pointed to herself as if to say, "Who, me?" I don't know who she is, but I felt love for her.

There were no words spoken from them.

Only *my* voice was audible.

I sat there for a while, and I was so thankful. This was an amazing experience that I will never forget.

Thank you, Kevin, for coming through again for me. I love you and I enjoy every moment I get spending time with you.

11/20/2019

I woke up at 3:30 am

I saw Kevin and it looked like he was talking to someone in his room. I then saw a guy walk out of his room. He just disappeared into the wall.

One after another on the wall I saw these funny cartoon images of pink cows and photos of people flashing by. It was like a photo album with the pages turning fast with people's faces. I didn't recognize any of the faces. I asked Kevin, who are they? Kevin started writing on the wall, but I could not read any of his messages they were fading too quickly, and they weren't clear enough.

I have no idea what he was trying to write to me. This has happened before where the writings are either missing vowels or they are in such a scribble like cursive that its almost unreadable.

11/27/2019

It was 5am when I woke up this morning. I saw Kevin and the blonde hair girl that he has been with him the last couple of times.

I saw them both projected on the same wall sitting by the beach, in the sand, on a blanket. Kevin loves the beach, and he had muscles like he used to have when he was working out religiously in High School. I get the impression that spirits are able to go anywhere they want. Spirits seem to enjoy all the same things in the afterlife as they did while here on earth.

Sometimes that's all I get. A quick flash of my sons face, his reassurance that he is okay.

12/07/2019

I woke up around 4:30am I saw a little girl sitting on Kevin's bed playing with Kevin's stuffed dog. I saw another blonde-haired lady. This lady was older and was wearing glasses. I have never seen this woman before.

There were other spirits around.

One man left from Kevin's room and looked straight at me. His face looked evil.

I felt scared, I did not like him. The presence of this spirit felt extremely negative, and he did not like me looking at him. This was my first time seeing a spirit that was not playful.

In my mind I said get out of my house! He pointed his hands at me with his fingers spread apart as if he was putting a curse on me. Then he disappeared.

Daylight started coming up and then they all were gone. I went back to sleep and woke up at 8 am to take Stella out. I went into Kevin's room I didn't see any spirits, but I assume that they could still hear me, so I started fussing out loud.

I was screaming no negative spirits are allowed in my house. Only my loved ones and positive spirits. As I was saying all of this to them, I got chills and goosebumps. To this day I have not seen that evil man again.

12/08/2019

I woke up around 430am I looked towards Kevin's room hoping to see him. I saw what looked like a 6 yr. old girl with light brown hair. Her hair was pulled back into a pink bow and she was wearing a white fluffy dress. There was also a little boy around 4 years old. His outfit was old looking. Maybe from another past decade. There was a toddler girl, and she was wearing a red corduroy dress. They were playing together in his room with his stuffed animals. Then they saw me and stopped playing and started waving and waving at me. They were smiling and happy to see me. I did not wave back, I was still upset about the other night, with that evil man, he really scared me. Seeing the other spirits, I was able to put my fear aside and communicate in the moment – though I was never really prepared (who really is) to see an entity that is evil.

The three of them were so cute, smiling and so happy they acted like they knew me, but I still could not bring myself to wave back at them. The three children moved from Kevin's room into my room by the door. I saw them very clear. They were still excited to see me, they wouldn't stop waving and smiling at me.

A man appeared in my room by my door also. He was wearing tan slacks. His clothing was from another time. It made me think of

1940s. He picked up the three kids and was holding them as they were still waving and so happy to see me.

I still could not wave back. I started talking in my head, asking," Who are you?" No response. Then they showed me a picture on the wall. it was a very old photo of the four of them. the sun started coming up and they all disappeared.

What could this mean? I felt bad as these kids acted like I was part of their life at some point., they felt love towards me – I was so mad at the "evil man" that my energy towards them was hindered due to the prior presence of him and the absence of my son Kevin.

12/10/2019
FLOATING ROSE

The spirits woke me up, I automatically looked into Kevin's room I didn't see any spirits. David was lying next to me, and I saw something by him, I thought it was his finger pointing up to the ceiling. I looked again and it wasn't his finger. This image was floating towards me. I think it was a rose and then it disappeared. I fell back to sleep and then woke up again. Stella was sleeping right next to me. I went to pet her and saw one single red rose, floating towards me. In that moment I thought to myself, Kevin is sending me a single red rose. A feeling of love filled my heart. I went to grab it, but I couldn't hold onto it. My hands went right through it.

I can see it floating in the air, but I can't feel it or touch it.

Unbelievable, everything is magical on the other side, and I am trying my best to learn and understand this gift.

12/28/19

Around 3am I suddenly woke up. I looked across and saw spirits in Kevin's room, by his door and in the hallway. As I laid in my bed, I watched my husband get up from the bed he headed towards the hallway and started walking downstairs. I say this, to you all because I am awake. I am able to distinguish from my sleep and my awake state of mind.

I thought for sure the spirits would all disappear, but they did not. David just walked right past them unaware and unbothered. I saw the spirit still there they didn't move, and he didn't see them. He came back upstairs, the spirits were still hanging around. I don't know why they didn't disappear this time, like they usually do. Therefore, I didn't say anything to David or the spirits to cause any disruption to my vision. I stayed up a little while longer hoping these spirits would bring Kevin though they did not and eventually they disappeared.

01/9/2020

At 6 AM in the morning I woke up. I saw Kevin appear in his room.

He jumped on his bed and did a flip in the air, not the tuck type of flip that you're thinking of.

His body was completely straight in a vertical position. I saw him flip in the air while in that stand-up vertical position. It was very quick.

Then he just glided through the walls and disappeared.

Through the years we've had several trampolines. My boys loved playing on them and soon became little professional backyard trampoline jumpers and flippers. They were so cute.

I love you and I miss you very much. Thank you for sending memories for me to see.

On my wall in the hallway, Kevin showed me a picture of a Titans football player. He had his hand stretched out, one leg up and one leg on the ground like he was trying to catch a football.

I said in my thoughts, "yes I know that's a Titan's player and they are playing tonight."

They are playing the Ravens who are the number one team in the playoffs the Titans are the underdog. I felt by that image Kevin gave me a sign that they were going to win tonight. I told Connor, David, and Michelle about it. David said if you believe that then bet them. So, I did, I bet the Titans straight up to win. This was my way of believing the sign I received and showing the spectators at the house that we already knew they were going to WIN! A few others also bet on the Titans. Good call from them.

The Titans made the first touchdown. and from there on they were in the lead the whole game. The Titans beat the Ravens. They shocked the world and knocked them out of the playoffs. Titans won 28-12.

Later that night I woke up and on the wall in the hallway I saw pictures in color of the Titans football team, Titans symbol, their flag and the Titans sign.

The wall was filled with nothing but Titan's stuff. It was like fireworks going off. I knew that was Kevin. He was here watching the game with us, and he was very excited. Connor was home and plus all of Kevin's friends were over to watch the game with us. We had so much fun all rooting for the Titans. We love you, Kevin. We are all rooting for your team. I know you were up there helping and watching us celebrate with you.

01/16/2020

I woke up, my wall was filled with Angels. They were all different sizes. They all had Angel wings and there was even a little Angel that was flapping her wings. It was a blessing to see all the different kinds of Angels.

01/20/2020
5:05 AM

I was in a deep sleep, and something woke me up. I looked directly into Kevin's room and saw him lying on his bed. He disappeared. I looked towards the wall and saw a Titans flag and a jersey.

Kevin was laying across the wall underneath them.

I saw wings. Angel wings flapping. The wings looked like they were flapping back and forth and coming from Kevin's back. This was my first time seeing him with Angel wings.

01/21/2020

I woke up at 6 am this morning and saw 3 Angels in the distance. I could tell it was two men and a woman. As they got closer to me, I saw that it was Kevin, he had his sunglasses on at first then he took them off in a movie style fashion. There was another guy alongside the same blonde hair girl. They started dancing in place all together in a straight line. While they were dancing, I saw words popping up on the wall. Same problems from before I could not read the writing. Instead, I stared at them while they danced. I saw that they all had angel wings on their back that were fluttering back and forth. Kevin had shown me he had angel wings yesterday. I see them so much more clearly fluttering back and forth. I am so proud of Kevin. I felt like he earned those wings from the expression on his face. I felt the excitement from him. All 3 of them seemed so excited to have those wings.

Kevin, keep sending me these signs and messages. I love you forever. Love never dies.

01/24/2020

Stella growled and woke me up at 7:15am. There I saw Kevin's handsome face smiling at me.

He was just beaming with happiness. He was on the wall by his big Titans banner in the corner by the window. I waved at him, he stretched both of his hands up towards the ceiling and gave me a big back-and forth wave. Then he faded off the wall. I went back to sleep as I woke up again, for the first time I felt a little happiness inside me.

Losing a child is the hardest thing anyone can face in their whole life. There is nothing worse in my life that will ever hurt me like this. But I am thankful that I am seeing all these precious gifts that God is giving me. I still have Kevin here and I have him in heaven he is watching over me, he is my special angel. I can see now that love never dies.

There is life after death.

01/25/2020

I don't know what time it was but all night long there was activity going on in Kevin's room. Here are some things the night brought me in raw format from my journal

I saw two women spirits conversing with each other and looking around. I saw the same blonde hair girl and she was giving one of the spirits a hug. Then Kevin appeared on the wall by his Titans banner in the corner next to the window. He was being funny with the girls, they were all talking to each other while laughing and smiling. I felt that I was watching a silent movie. Kevin noticed that I was awake and saw me looking at him. With his lips he mouthed. I love you mom.

I was shocked to see him move his mouth in such a slow and understandable way that communicated better to me than the writings on the wall. I got the message clear as day.

I love you too Kevin.

When I said I love you too it was in my thoughts. This is easier to convey than talking out loud. I at once felt overflowing emotional love, and this comforts me. I couldn't keep my eyes off him. He was looking at me and I was looking back. He waved at me, and I waved back. I fell back to sleep watching them in the room enjoying themselves. The next time I woke up I saw drawings of bouquets of flowers on the wall like they were etched in black pencil. There was a message and it said "Look what I can do".

In my thoughts I told Kevin how proud I am of him all the signs he is giving me he's doing a great job over there. I love how you communicated to me with your mouth compared to writings. I love you so much.

Then looking into Kevin's room, I saw something on the ceiling slowly come out of his room as onto the wall. It was a pencil sketched star attached to a bouquet of flowers. Then I saw something else floating out of his room in front of the wall. it was a sign that said "Yours". The phrase "Yours" was coming towards me. Is Kevin saying I'm always going to be "Yours"?

It is unbelievable how Kevin and I are communicating. I love it. God answered my prayers.

01/28/2020

It was 2:30 AM I woke up and saw two Spirit girls sitting on Kevin's bed bouncing a baby girl. The baby was wearing a red dress had brown hair and brown eyes.

They were smiling and having a good time with her. They looked up and saw me and they started clapping their hands. I actually heard the sounds of the spirits clapping.

This was the first time I have ever heard a sound while awake. Prior to this it was visual writings on the wall, or a sound that would wake me up. As mentioned, Kevin mouthed words with his lips a few days prior.

The two girls started waving at me and turned the baby around for me to see and she waved at me too she was so cute. I noticed a spirit behind them which was Kevin. David had woken up and turned on the light in the bathroom and they all disappeared.

02/2/2020

Tonight, I saw a bunch of spirits. I believe there is some sort of portal there in Kevin's room on the wall where his Titans flag hangs. The spirits feel free to come through there.

I saw a female spirit greeting other spirits as they were coming through.

I got the feeling that they were coming to celebrate, or it was an awards night. I looked over to the wall and saw photos of the same people that I have seen before on the wall. It resembles a photo album.

I do not know who any of those people are, but they are the same ones in those photos that they keep showing me over and over again.

02/4/2020

Even though I have been able to see my son and communicate with him, I still walk around day to day carrying an overwhelming amount of pain and grief. This is all bigger than me and what my human body can handle. It is so hard to be a human and deal with all these emotions. I believe that God, Kevin, my guardian angels, and the other spirits are all here to carry me through this new reality that I have been faced with. Somewhere inside of me I know that I will learn to live with the loss of Kevin and focus on the gift that he was and still is to me.

David and I went to this pub today. We always took Kevin with us to play the slot machines and spend time together. I was telling David how much I loved Kevin's tattoos on his arm.

That night when I went to bed spirits woke me up and I saw a quick close-up of Kevin's face. Then I saw his whole body he was stretching his arms out above his head which I thought was unusual, he normally would waved at me.

Then I realize he was showing me the arm with the tattoos that I love.

Kevin is always with us no matter where we are.

To me that was a validation.

How else was he aware that we had a full on conversation about his beautiful tattoos? This left me with a peaceful feeling inside. I fell back into a deep sleep and got some much needed rest. Thank you, Kevin,

02/14/2020
HAPPY VALENTINE'S DAY

Today Kevin sent me a Valentines gift. When I woke up there was a big Valentines heart with red and pink flowers on the inside of the heart. It was so sharp and clear. It was beautiful.

The only words I saw were "I love you". I still couldn't read the rest of the words, but I thought I got the most important message he was sending. I love you.

Thank you, Kevin,

02/16/2020

I really believe things on the other side are like they are here from what I've been shown. It's much more magical than I could have ever imagined. I saw Kevin with another lady and a little boy about 4-5 years old. they were standing up holding a wood frame. He was pointing at it, he seemed very proud and wanted me to see that he received an award plaque. All three of them waved at me and of course I waved back.

Congratulations on this award

We are so proud of you.

02/18/2020

There was Kevin and another guy coming through the portal which is in his room. He was dancing as he was coming through.

I sat up in bed and then everything disappeared.

I laid back down and fell asleep.

Later, when I woke up again, I saw more spirits coming through the portal. This time, I got a glimpse of another room which looked like a big banquet room. There were a lot of spirits in that room socializing. They were sitting at long tables, some were getting up and dancing. I saw Kevin as I watched him get up to dance, he had some good dancing moves, he was laughing and playing around, spirits were all around him.

He was the life of the party. Just like he was here on earth.

Then he looked over and saw me, he started dancing towards the portal. He looked so happy,

He was having a great time. Once he came through the portal into his room, he waved to me and I waved back.

Then all of a sudden everything vanished.

I laid there in my bed, wishing Kevin was still here with all of us.

He was our life of the party.

I closed my eyes and went back to sleep.

I woke up again, this time I saw a lady spirit in a yellow dress walking out of Kevin's room and she immediately disappeared. Then I saw another lady spirit with blonde hair.

She also was coming out of Kevin's room heading towards the hallway railings.

I couldn't see her face, but I heard her say, "Hi Melodi" I was in shock. Her voice sounded just like my Aunt Glenda. This was the second time I actually heard a spirit speak. I replied "hi". I don't know who she was, but she said my name and I heard that. This is a breakthrough for me. I wanted to learn how to communicate with words and this week I heard Kevin talk to me and now another spirit talking to me. I am embracing whatever God gives me I want to learn. I'm open and I'm ready. I praise the Lord for all the special moments. I love you God.

MARCH 2020

I forgot to mention that our cat died January 6, 2020

This cat came to us in 2009.

She appeared on our deck. She had no collar or tags, but she was fixed.

Kevin wanted to feed her. I said, "No if you feed cats they never leave". His friend said, "Don't worry Mrs. Shipley she's going to die from starvation anyway."

That upset Kevin so much, he said, "Mom we have to feed her we can't let her starve." From there on we fed her, fixed a place for her to sleep at on the deck. We took care of her for over 10 years.

RIP our Kitty Cat.

She was a very good cat and we loved her.

Since then, I have seen her in spirit once in Kevin's room and once in my room.

I also saw a black miniature horse with our cat, chickens, and ducks in my bedroom.

Within a matter of seconds, they all disappeared.

I have been seeing animals, babies, toddlers, kids, and adults all in Kevin's room, in the hallway and my room.

I did see Kevin he looked at me, his mouth was moving he was trying to say something. I heard his voice, but I could not hear what he was actually saying.

I saw Kevin again in his room this time he was laying on his bed taking a Selfie.

He didn't see me until after he took his selfie. He looked up and saw me and then he disappeared.

I don't see Kevin all the time, but I do see spirits and some of them are beginning to be the same ones. I'm still waiting to see my dad. I have been praying but he has not appeared yet.

03/10/2020

Early morning, I saw Kevin's face and neck through the railings of the stairs next to his door. Therefore, I couldn't see his face too clear. He had his beats headphones on again which he loved, and his head was bobbing back and forth. He was listening to his music at the same time he was texting on his cellphone like he did when he was home on earth.

Who is he texting?

He looked up saw me and waved an then went back to his music and phone. They do whatever they want.

There were spirits in his room. This one lady had a notebook in her hands like she was taken notes. She was walking fast out of his room heading towards my room and then flew straight up to the ceiling and disappeared.

03/11/2020

I laid there for a while meditating. I took deep breaths and relaxed my entire body state. I started to hear music in my head from afar. As I was meditating, I saw three circles of bright white lights. Two of the lights blended into each other making it one light. I'm not sure of what all of this means. I'm taking it all in. One day I will understand.

03/15/2020

Every night I look into Kevin's room to see what I can see. Sometimes I see nothing, but most of the time I can see everything. This time this is what I saw:

Laying in my room was a tiger with her baby laying in front of her. I saw a present wrapped in burlap with a burlap ribbon leaning on the railing. The tiger and her baby disappeared but the present was still there until I fell asleep. My visions aren't limited to what I know, in fact it's usually what I don't know. In this case I am unaware of why I saw these animals and what the present left truly meant. I am learning.

04/3/2020

David woke up around 2 am in the morning to go downstairs to sleep.

I went back to sleep, but not for long what I saw was a happy hour.

There were several spirits in Kevin's room and in the hallway. They were mixing and mingling as if they were in a Bar. I saw spirits coming through the portal being greeted by other spirits as they came through.

My eyes were burning, sometimes they get like that when I see spirits.

I was trying to focus in on them as much as I could.

Then I saw the same regular blonde hair girl. Kevin was peeking around the corner. His hair was longer, he had a beard and a mustache. He looked just like he does on the cover of my book.

He walked over to sit down at the bar that actually was the headboard on his bed.

The atmosphere was set up like being at a bar. They were standing up, seating down and had drinks in their hands, it was a fun site to see.

Two male spirits came from the portal who went and stood next to Kevin. They were wearing face masks like we are for COVID -19.

The first impression I got was that they wanted to let me know they know what is going on down here.

04/07/2020

All this time I was thinking that my son was drawing all the images on my wall.

To my surprise what I saw last night has made me change my mind. I was very restless, tossing and turning. Something woke me up. I looked and there on the wall were drawings of cartoon figures.

They were drawn with colored chalk. The images started dancing around as I started to focus more. I saw a group of 5 kids kneeling down by the railings in the hallway and giggling. That's when I realized they drew and colored those cartoon pictures that came alive. They were looking at me and I gave them a thumbs up. They started laughing they were so excited.

They begin waving, smiling, and clapping. I was filled with excitement they made me happy I was waving, smiling and clapping with them.

I knew for sure they did these drawings for me. I know that Kevin sends me writings, words, and messages on the wall. Even though I see other spirits I didn't realize they are sending messages directly to me also.

Wow! A lot is going on. There is so much to learn.

04/19/2020

I saw our old Kitty Cat again by my red lounge chair in my room. She was playing with the tassels on my blanket. I saw a white shadow /cloud or maybe a spirit hovering above and over the cat. Then it dropped into the cat and they both disappeared.

08/14/2020
5:00 AM

On the wall that I call my "movie projector wall" I saw a bundle of money, stacked up all over the wall.

It reminded me what you would see in a bank vault. There was a male spirit in the middle of all this money and he was throwing it at me. I believe this is a good sign for me.

08/16/2020
4:30AM

My eyes literally saw Kevin appear in his room. He looked at me and waved. He stood up and started strumming his guitar. I would of love to hear what he was playing.

Then just like that Kevin vanished.

I went back to sleep.

I believe that Kevin woke me up.

On the wall by my mirror there was a page from a music book. It had musical notes and then underneath there were letters.

I couldn't read or understand the lyrics. I need to learn what these signs mean.

There are much more writings on the wall that I just can't remember.

I'm happy that I'm remembering some of things though nothing compares to being able to see Kevin.

Thank you, dear God, for this gracious gift.

Today I went to a spiritual healing class. This was my first time trying Reiki.

They had 3 message beds set up in one of the rooms. We laid down on our back on the beds and close our eyes with a sleep mask on. I was relaxed and comfortable.

There were healers for each person. They used a pendulum, crystals and prayers to open up our Chakras.

I laid there, while she scanned my whole body.

She told me that my heart weighs very heavy and it is broken.

There is a lot of energy in the heart area that needs to be healed.

She described a thin young man in his 20s with brown hair kind of wavy parted to the side. A goatee and a mustache, nice looking young man who is funny. Had suddenly appeared right next to me.

He gave her a thumbs up when she was scanning me.

With a chuckle to her voice, she said, I don't understand this, he said.

"Let the bodies hit the floor."

I said, "OMG, That is my son Kevin!!!! Who has passed away.

He would say something like that.

Plus, he listens to that song, it's on his playlist.

I am so familiar with that song. I got goosebumps and I started crying. She said that he told her that he loves me very much.

He is always around me, but he wants me to start living life.

He told her that he always comes when I need him and call on him. But sometimes he might not be able to come because he has other obligations on the other side.

She was saying more, but I couldn't comprehend everything she was saying, I was so amazed of what she had already picked up on. The lady that was the healer was new, and she did an impressive job.

What an experience.

She would never of known to guess a song like that.

She gave me the perfect validation.

For some reason I sleep through the whole night.

I woke up early in the morning.

I at once saw Kevin's face on the wall.

I was so grateful and happy all at the same time to see him so quickly.

Thank you, Kevin, I knew you would come to the healing class. I love you.

He just made my whole day by seeing his happy face

He also validated that he was with me that night.

I am so blessed to have these signs and to see him.

Thank you, dear God.

10/16/2020

Today is Kevin's birthday.

I laid in my bed to meditate. I was asking for Kevin to come visit me.

In my meditation, I saw my son Connors face. Then I saw Kevin sneakily walk behind Connor in the kitchen. He walked over and sat down at the kitchen table, and he smiled at me. He flashed both of his hands up with all 10 fingers twice and then 9 fingers the third time. He is 29 today. I saw big white clouds, and, in the clouds, I saw the number

29 and a big red heart. He looked at me with his beautiful smile and waved goodbye.

He is always with us.

I saw white clouds moving around I saw the colors green, purple and deep blue moving around like clouds. Then the white clouds opened, and I saw a Big White Light. Could that have been Kevin?

01/11/2021

At night, I saw in Kevin's room, 12 young adult spirits, both men, and women. There were 3 rows, and they were sitting 4 to a row, it reminded me of auditorium seating or something similar to a jury. As soon as the spirits realized I saw them they all stood up.

I felt that they were giving me a standing ovation. All of them were smiling, laughing, and clapping with excitement.

They made me feel very special.

I had this overwhelming feeling of love for all of them. So much so that this experience remains very unique for me.

I was waving both of my hands at them, and it felt like I knew them and missed them. They were greeting me with happiness and love. I also in return did the same. This lasted for a brief but unforgettable moment. The encouragement and all around energy was very positive.

All together they flew up so fast to the ceiling and disappeared. Their exit was so fast however I noticed wings on the back of one of them.

I wondered if they were my angels and guides? This was the first time that I felt a connection with the spirits other than my son.

02/15/21

As I was getting into my bed, I was pulling my blanket closer to me.

I saw right in front of me this white steam coming towards me and then it began floating around me. It flowed out of my hands and up out of my fingertips. It was mesmerizing.

I thought could this be energy? Or were they my angels around me?

MARCH 2021

If I hadn't been experiencing spirits for the last two years, I would have jumped out of my bed screaming my lungs out. This experience happened. I was in a deep sleep.

I felt something rub across gently on my cheek, which woke me up. I saw a wrist, hand and a pointer finger strumming my face so softly as I laid there. It resembled the hand from the Addams Family. Immediately the hand quickly moved away and into my bed post.

I wasn't scared because I knew it was Kevin's hand and he just wanted to let me know that everything is going to be ok

I love you my son

08/20/2021

I woke up this morning and, in my mirror, I saw a male spirit with a baseball cap on. He started coming closer to the glass on the mirror. Other spirits were behind him closely following him in the mirror. They all spread out across filling up the mirror space and started clapping. They were all raising their hands as if they were cheering me on. It was one big celebration.

It just so happened today is the day I finished all the chapters in my book. I'm now ready for the next stages.

CHAPTER 7

VOICES FROM HEAVEN

Things keep happening to me. I don't understand all of it. I'm just embracing everything that's coming my way. I like to share with you all the voices that I'm hearing.

I believe are from heaven.

A couple days right before Mother's
Day May 2019. I heard Kevin's voice.
My eyes automatically look up to the
ceiling that is where it sounded like it
was coming from. It sounded far away,
but I heard him say
I Love You Mom!! I Love You Mom!!!

I knew what I heard. I was overwhelmed with excitement I started to shout back "I love you too Kevin, I love you, I love you."

I kept saying it over and over. I needed to make sure he could hear me. Every sign that I get I let him know that I got it so he will continue to communicate with me in every way.

OCTOBER 2020

It was early in the morning,

I was laying in my bed by myself thinking about Kevin. I miss and love him so much. I was trying to relax so I could do some meditation. I heard music playing, I didn't have the radio on in my house. I sat up in my bed trying to listen to what the song was saying.

This is what I heard:

I still love you; I still love you,
Even though I'm far away.
Don't you worry.
Don't you worry.
Don't you worry anymore
I'm here with you.

The song was repeating these words several times. Then the music stopped playing.

I believe this was sent from heaven

11/18/2020
9.17AM

I was lying in my bed sleeping when I heard a voice that woke me up, it sounded like Martin Luther King Jr. He was speaking the way he would talk at his rallies. I couldn't catch everything he was saying., but this is what I heard:

It's going to be another revolution; they are trying to control the government.

There's going to be a WAR. And when I say war, I mean nuclear war.

I was trying to listen to hear more because they were just going on and on. I thought David had the TV on. I got up to go downstairs because I wanted to hear what they were saying. I thought I was hearing the news. He had a TV show on, and the volume was very low. I asked him if he was watching the news, he said, no. I told him what I was hearing, and he said I was dreaming. I heard voices! I wasn't dreaming because I was up in bed trying to listen to what they were saying thinking the news was on.

I went back upstairs to lay down.

I closed my eyes and started to meditate. I saw a record player with a record playing backwards on the turntable.

In the background there were pictures of the of the past rewinding back, Then I saw a younger me in the kitchen sitting at the table with Kevin as a little boy on my lap. He was about 7 years old.

I was enjoying being back in the past with my son again.

What kind of messages do you think this is?

11/20/2020
7:30AM

I heard a male voice singing what sounded like heavy rock. It started softly then got louder and I began to hear some words in a scratchy voice say

"There's no one I'd rather be with than you. "

The voice repeated the words over and over again.

MARCH 2021

I'm gonna love you.
Till the heavens stop the rain.
I'm gonna love you,
Till the stars fall from the sky for you, and I

For some reason when I woke up- I started singing this song, I was in tune '" surprise'" however I didn't know the song or even who sang it at first. This went on for weeks, Finally, I decided to look it up on the internet. The song is called "Touch Me" by The Doors.

This was the same month when I had the hand reach out and touch me on my face. (See Chapter 6 spirits)

"Come on, come on, come on, come on now touch me, babe Can't you see that I am not afraid?

Thank you, Kevin I am not afraid I love you

08/16/2021

I heard these voices which I believe are messages from heaven. I wasn't able to write them all down though these are what I was able to recall.

"I just want you to know that I love you."

"The sun comes up, the sun goes down I'm all around you, most of the time."

"You'll dream the rest of your life."

12/05/2021

I didn't want to get up, it was one of those mornings where I just laid there feeling very sad for myself missing my son. I started to get emotional until I heard a voice. It was Kevin, so I stopped crying to tune in to the message and this is what I heard

"Raise your Energy"

"Mom! Raise your Energy"
"Mom!! Raise your Energy"

MARCH 2022

This is what I heard that woke me up.

"I love you,"
"Mom!! I love you"
"Mom!!! I really, really love you."

That voice was my son, he was
strumming on a guitar and singing to
me.
I was surprised that he was playing the guitar and singing at the
same time.
It was so beautiful.

What a nice way to wake up.

He wanted to make sure I could hear him.
I can hear you Kevin, I can hear you.
I love you too.

APRIL 2022

As I was sleeping, I heard a knock that woke me up. It was early morning, day light was coming through.
I heard a female voice whisper softly,

We love you very much.
We love you very much.

We love you very much

She said it over and over again
I responded saying who are you?
As they kept on saying,
we love you very much.

At that moment, I felt a sense of love come over me, a feeling
of knowing.

Are you, my angels?
I said, I can hear you.
I love you all too very much.

I'm starting to hear more voices as time goes on.
Thank you, Dear God,
I love all the gifts you have giving to me.

CHAPTER 8

ASTRAL TRAVEL

Astral travel is when you have
a spiritual out of body experience

I've been reading a lot about Astral Traveling. From what I have read if you align and raise your energy to a certain frequency, with the help of meditation, you will be able to break through and venture into higher realms or the spiritual world.

I have been praying for a chance to astral travel.

02/9/2020

As I laid down in my bed for the night, I looked across the hall into Kevin's room to see if he is there. He was not.

I dozed off into a deep asleep.

I had a dream, that my husband and I were laying in our bed, however there were other people in our room laying in separate beds which resembled something similar to a hospital, these people were waiting to see the doctor. I got up and went into Kevin's Room which didn't look like his room at all. His walls were covered with posters top to bottom and there were random people/spirits in his room. There was one guy laying on Kevin's bed and he was looking at Kevin's pokemon cards and stealing some of them. I did not like them going through Kevin's stuff. I saw two ladies which I got the impression were nurses and I told them that I don't mind if people are coming to my house to see the doctor, but I don't want them messing with my sons' stuff or stealing anything. I told them very sternly if they don't take care of this behavior, I will kick everybody out. Then suddenly bam, I was back in my bedroom, and everyone was gone, and my dream was over.

After I woke up, I grabbed some water to gather myself from that wild dream. I decided to lay back down and here is where things changed.

What happened next is hard for me to describe.

I felt an extreme force come over me and it jolted my body across my bed.

Have you ever gotten on the ride at the carnival called the scrambler? This is how it felt as my body was moving from side to side. I had no control over my body movements.

I ended up hitting against my husband while he was sleeping and then I got pushed back to the other side of the bed. I had no control.

I felt an even more intense shock which had arched my back and I levitated out of my physical body. I floated to the ceiling and realized I now was only my soul.

I was not afraid which I believe allowed me to move freely. At that moment from all the reading and praying I have done I knew I cross over the veil and was astral traveling. I floated through the ceiling and down into Kevin's room.

The feeling I got going into Kevin's room was similar to being on a roller coaster.

As I floated into his room, I saw Kevin laying in his bed sleeping with his Titans' blanket around him.

To me he looked so real. I was stunned to see him up close and personal.

I moved closer to be next to him and he woke up. He looks so surprise to see me, more like shocked.

He had short hair and a clean-shaven face. A white T-shirt on. He looked at me and I looked at him. I moved in even closer and held his hand under his blanket. This felt so real. It felt like my son was still alive. I could feel the warmth and the bone on his hand.

In that moment, I was speechless. I felt like I was star struck by my own son. Nothing felt as real as this moment before. I didn't know what to say. I sat there in awe for seconds until I was able to speak.

Still being star struck- I asked him," how are you doing. His lips were moving back and forth but I couldn't hear anything instead, I felt his words say to me

"Mom go back into your box"

I said why?

He said you're hurting my hand. Let me show you. He uncovered his hand the one I was holding under the blanket.

There was a glowing fireball of light around our hands. I did not feel a thing. I saw bright colors of red, yellow, and orange swirling around I let go of his hand immediately. He said it again to me,

" Mom go back in your box"

I didn't want to go. I didn't want to leave. I wanted to visit my son. I wanted to talk to him.

The look in his eyes made me say OK and in a split second I was on my way floating back to my bed like a Genie in a bottle. The same roller coaster feeling happened again.

As I approached my body, my physical eyes started to open. To the left of me I noticed an Angel on the side of my bed. The impression I got seemed like he was not only protecting me but making sure I got back into my physical body safely. He disappeared once I was in and fully in control of my body.

When I got back into my body, I was very hot and sweaty. I sat there for a moment just thinking of what had happened to me. This was the most fascinating experience I have ever had.

I praise God and thank God for this wonderful journey. I really believe I was on the other side. I crossed over the veil. I'm praying that this experience will happen again and again. I absolutely loved it and I thank you dear God for all these beautiful gifts.

04/02/2020

I believe I had another astral travel. Although this was different from the first one, I experienced. What was similar is I felt like I was coming out of my body again, so as it was happening, I extended my arms reaching towards the ceiling which to me looked like the sky. As I began to rise. I embraced the feeling expecting something magical.

I saw a beautiful bright white cloud and I was going through it with my eyes closed (or could this have been my third eye?). It was amazing I could feel my momentum pushing me through the clouds.

Then I broke through the clouds and I had this falling sensation as I landed in a room that I have never seen before. There was a man and a woman waiting there for me. While in that room my body was very hard for me to control. My legs felt rubbery, and I couldn't stand up or walk. The man and woman in the room both had to hold me up. They were trying to get me to the couch to sit down

I heard them say "We need to get her energy down. She is hot."

I said to the woman, "I almost made it to the other side, but I opened my eyes".

She said to me "that's Ok you have plenty of time."

Then everything disappeared - the next thing I knew I was by myself just walking along a college campus with students. Suddenly I saw Kevin, he was running towards me, and I started running towards him as fast as I could.

I was screaming "Kevin Kevin!!!

We ran into each other's arms. He wrapped them around me and gave me the biggest hug. He was weeping with tears running down his cheeks telling me "I miss you all so much". I was crying uncontrollably telling him how much we miss him, and how we love him so much.

I could see everything so incredibly clear. He looked just like the handsome man he is with his thin mustache and little goatee. When I held him, he felt human just like before in my first Astral Travel. He was alive again. I could feel my son.

With all this glory in the moment – still my heart was shattered knowing I cannot bring my son back home with me.

We sat down on the hill at the campus, and I held his hands and asked him what he was doing.

He said to me, "I have been very busy and what I do is help young spirits transition over and take them where they need to be.

I gave him another big hug and a kiss and then sadly I watched him glide away.

I came back to my physical body, but I didn't want to leave. I wish I had more time to spend with him.

In that moment after astral traveling, I reflected on my experience. I was very emotional, but my body was relaxed. I couldn't move a muscle. I just laid there thinking about what just happened.

Thank you, dear God,

06/23/20
5:30 AM

Stella woke up and David took her out to potty. I glanced at the clock and realized it was still early. I fell back into a deep sleep, and then I got that floating feeling again. Here I was coming out of my body with that jolt. I could feel the excitement in me as I floated through the wall and ceiling of my room. That roller coaster feeling was back. I was astral traveling. The whole time I was levitating up I was thanking God for letting me experience this again. I love this feeling.

This time I landed in a building which looked like an old school. There were double doors that were green, and I started wandering around.

I walked out into the hallway and there was a lady passing by, and I asked her if she knew where Kevin Shipley was? She said "yes, follow me" so I followed her into those green double doors. When she opened the doors up there were tables like a school cafeteria

When I say people were sitting there, I mean spirits. These spirits all were sitting at the tables as if they were eating but I did not see any food.

The lady pointed to where Kevin was, so I walked towards him. He looked right up and saw me coming over. We both were so excited to see each other.

I sat across from him at the table. He looked great; his chest was wide with his big muscles. I said have you been working out? He gave me a smirk.

I asked him how he was doing, and what other things were going on over here.

Then the cafeteria turned into a big field. There were spirits all around us. He was excited and happy to be in this field.

He was looking at them smiling and he said to me they all are being reincarnated. They will be going back to Earth.

I said to him "maybe they will let you come back if you want to". He said "no I cannot come back now" I said why not? "Did you ask them?"

Then just like that we were back in the original school building again.

Kevin said to me I am going to see Aunt Lillie now. She had passed away two months before Kevin in 2019.

I said to him "Let's go!"

After I said that, I felt a weird feeling like I was getting ready to leave the astral travel, and I said aloud "No I'm not ready to go back I want to see Aunt Lillie". That feeling of leaving disappeared and I stayed in my astral projection.

Kevin opened the double green doors and inside was a bed and people were gathered all around a woman. This lady did not look like our Aunt Lillie. She was noticeably young, and she had brown hair with a bowl haircut. I don't know who she was, but it was supposed to be my aunt.

We walked back into the main hallway of the building, and I started feeling like I was in two places at the same time. I could feel part of me going back to my body. but I also was face-to-face with Kevin, and I asked him are you happy? He said "Yes". Then he looked at me again and said, "sometimes I am sad mom." This broke my heart even more.

Everything disappeared.

I was now back in my body. This time I did not see myself coming back into my body nor did I see any spirit watching as I entered my body. It all happened so fast.

Later that day, I was out lounging by my pool pondering over what really happened to me.

I felt that when I astral travel, I reach another dimension on the other side of the veil.

In that very moment of my thought, a red cardinal flew out in front of me and landed into the tree. The cardinal stared at me and started chirping.

I called my niece Michelle that evening and as I was telling her everything that happened to me today. When I got to the part about the Cardinal. There was a moment of silent, she said to me "Aunt Melodi there is a cardinal flying by my window right now!"

Amazing.

To me, this was a sign from my son.

He confirmed that I did astral travel, I did cross the veil to the other side, and I am aware.

I thank you God for all these beautiful experiences.

I love you, Kevin.

08/31/2020
6:54AM

Stella woke me up from a deep sleep. My husband came upstairs to get her. As I was falling back to sleep, I started seeing clouds that were big and small with blue skies, the clouds became swirls of colors, orange, green, and white expanding and contracting.

I felt closeness to these clouds. My body started tingling from my toes and working its way up. I was very relaxed.

I wanted to reach the clouds. I wanted to follow the clouds. they were coming and going, and the color changes were popping in and out. In between all the clouds an angel with two big white wings on his back appeared. His shape was that of a young man's body. This beautiful angel didn't make any eye contact with me he just walked by and blended in with the clouds. I knew he was one of my angels. I felt he wanted me to know that he was with me.

I felt my whole body relax into almost feeling numb.

I made sure I didn't open my eyes.

In my thoughts I kept saying I want to visit Kevin and I would love to astral travel again. I wanted to explore and learn more and more about the other side. I was ready to go.

I felt myself being released from my body as I was rising in my thoughts, I was saying I want to see Kevin over and over again. I started to fly. what an awesome feeling. I love it.

I landed in a place that I knew was supposed to be our home, but it didn't look like our house that we live in. Kevin appeared. I was so excited to see him. We hugged and kissed.

It felt like he was back at home with me, and we were home. But this was not our house. Kevin looked older and more mature. He was wearing a white t-shirt, a casual blazer jacket and tan pants.

He was an extremely handsome grown up man. I got the feeling that he was home to stay. He was alive. I could feel him. I was so happy that he was alive again and could come back home.

I knew he had died, but it felt like he didn't. I thought God gave him a second chance, it was that real. He was smiling and I felt blessed I had my son back.

I gave Kevin another big hug and kiss and I held onto him, I was not going to let go... I didn't want to lose him again. then he started walking away and I grievously watched him go. There was nothing I could do. I couldn't stop him. I felt myself going back into my body it was quick and fast.

I stayed asleep.

Thank you, Dear God,
for
The Gift of KEVIN

EPILOGUE

ANGELS CALLING

11/29/2021

Several weeks before this happened,
  I was praying to God, more like questioning what my purpose is here on this earth and unsure of everything that's going on in my life.

I went upstairs to go to bed. I closed my eyes and started seeing white clouds moving all around, In between all these clouds I saw 3 little white angels with wings on the back flying in and out. Then I fell into a deep sleep.

I heard a knock-knock sound which made me open up my eyes.

I saw a long pole, reminded me of a curtain rod. Hanging on it was a washcloth that had a red rose design. On top of the rod was a statue of an owl which was next to the rose wash cloth.

The word Wolf spelled out was next to the owl, they all were line up together. The rod was floating towards me, with all of them in line on the rod.

As it got closer to me, it disappeared and then I saw spirits in my mirror waving with excitement at me, then they also disappeared.

I look into Kevin's room didn't see him, but I saw the word Wolf spelled out on his wall.

I knew at this point; this was definitely a message.

What does it mean? I don't know, but I will find out.

I fell back into a deep sleep which turn into a dream. I saw a flame of fire (like a lighter) went off in my face which made me jump, it scared me, now I woke up.

My eyes went directly to the clock. This was the time on the clock 11:11.

Now I know this is a message from my angels.

I know about the angel numbers, but now I need to find out what the owl and the word wolf means.

This is what I found out.

We all know what the Red Rose means to me.
A sign that love lasts forever and can never die.
Eternal unbreakable bond.

The Owl is often seen as a messenger from the spirit realm. Owls have been associated with bringing one wisdom, truth, and helping one understand life's mysteries.

The Wolf is also seen as a spirit animal for protection of the family alongside freedom and keeping your spirit alive.

11:11 are angel numbers and your spirit guides are attempting to contact you.

This is a spiritual awakening that you are aligned and on the right path for your soul's purpose.

God and all the angels are
always with us no matter what.

Written and spoken by

KEVIN SHIPLEY

JUNE 3, 2012

EVEN WHEN IT SEEMS AS THOUGH ALL
HOPE IS LOST, AND THERE IS NO WAY TO
CARRY ON, YOU MUST REALIZE THAT IT
IS NOT THE END YET.
HOPE IS STILL OUT THERE SOMEWHERE,
AND IT'S UP TO YOU TO LOOK FOR IT.
WHEN DARKNESS FALLS AND THE LIGHT
FLEES, YOUR HEART MUST SHINE AND
YOUR SOUL MUST STRENGTHEN.
YOU MUST WILL YOURSELF TO CARRY
ON, EVEN IN THE DARKEST OF TIMES.
IN THE END, NOT ALL WILL BE LOST,
AND LIFE WILL BE BEAUTIFUL ONCE AGAIN.

TO ALL MY READERS

THANK YOU

I hope you have enjoyed reading about the spiritual journey I have been on so far and all the supernatural experiences I have had since losing my amazing son Kevin. My wish for you, the reader, is that you understand life down here is only temporary. Our true purpose is well beyond the small amount of time we spend here on earth.

We all have our own unique journey to complete and our own lessons to learn down here. Nobody said it would be easy but try to open your mind and find the beauty in both life and death. Just believe.

Our loved ones will never truly leave us when they cross over to the other side. No matter what, they are always watching over us and guiding us in our times of need.

To me, losing a child has been the most painful thing one can go through.

I wrote this book for me. I needed to express myself and journal these supernatural experiences. Expressing these feelings and emotions has not been easy

I do not know what I would be doing right now if I did not throw all my sorrow and pain into my book.

I was always a strong positive person, but when I lost my amazing and beautiful child, I was too broken to stay strong and I too questioned my own beliefs.

I just want you all to know that even after all that has happened, I still feel the love. On the other side his soul is well alive, and he is happy.

Trust in the signs you will receive from your loved ones. Be open to them. Pray for them to come to you. Once you awaken yourself to these endless possibilities you will receive more signs.

This book helps me keep his spirit and legacy alive.

This book gave me something more to do than just cry every day.

I poured my heart and soul into this book, and I am hoping that it brings a different outlook to life.

I want you to know that you are not alone, and you will once again find the strength to smile and laugh once again. When you are ready of course.

My endless love and appreciation to all of you.

-Melodi Shipley

GOD BLESS